ONE STOP
MARKETING

ONE STOP MARKETING

JONATHAN TRIVERS

John Wiley & Sons, Inc.

New York • Chichester • Brisbane • Toronto • Singapore

Copyright © 1996 by Jonathan Trivers
Published by John Wiley & Sons, Inc.

Library of Congress Cataloging-in-Publication Data:

Trivers, Jonathan.
    One stop marketing / Jonathan Trivers.
        p.   cm.
    Includes bibliographical references.
    ISBN 0–471–13331–0 (cloth : alk. paper).—ISBN 0–471–13332–9
(pbk. : alk. paper)
    1. Marketing.   I. Title.
    HF5415.T713   1996
    658.8—dc20   95–52903
                                                               CIP

Printed in the United States of America

10 9 8 7 6 5 4 3 2 1

*For my wife, Karen, and our brood, John Michael,
Kelly, Robert, Conor, and Nathan.
The children thought the only thing I could write was
checks, reluctantly. Now what do you think?*

CONTENTS

ACKNOWLEDGMENTS

Thanks to my early readers and advisers. Jenni Haas was my very first reader and supporter. My brother, Dr. Robert Trivers, a noted evolutionary biologist (Ph.D., Harvard) read the manuscript, changed the classified ad he was running for his 1978 Toyota to better reflect his new marketing wisdom, and sold the clunker to the first caller. My sister, Mildred, uses her newfound marketing knowledge to train GM employees. Good luck! David Palmer helped me find and cut off dangerous dangling participles and wayward gerunds. Judy Fitzgerald, Mandy Oliveira, and Roger Harding gave me their small business perspective.

Thanks to my agent, Binky Urban. Binky liked the book and laughed. Thanks to John Stearns who forced me to write "lean."

Thanks to Mike Hamilton, Senior Editor at John Wiley & Sons. He cajoled, pushed, and prodded to make a better book than I thought I could produce.

Special thanks to my wife, Karen. She supported this venture, helped me learn how to use our word processor, and, when all else failed, came up with this marvelous title. Thanks mutti.

J.C.T.

INTRODUCTION

This book is fun. Marketing is the most exciting part of running a Main Street retail store. My style is to get you to smile and learn, in that order.

One Stop Marketing is simple. The best marketing ideas are simple and obvious. We all know that the customer decides our business fate. The logical extension of that is: Since the customer decides, why not let them lead? If you listen to your customers and actively solicit their advice, they will become advocates for your store and find more customers like themselves. And the cycle of success never stops.

This book is real-life marketing. I share with you many stories of retail success and failure of Main Street retailers. You might not recognize their stores, but you will understand their challenges.

THE CHANGING CUSTOMER

One Stop Marketing is for the small business that is selling to the consumer market. It is about customers—how to find and keep them. Finding and keeping customers has always been the fundamental aim of marketing, but today's customers are different than the "traditional" customers of the 1970s and early 1980s. There is no broad, easily definable middle group for taste, values, and consumption. Since the mid-1970s, America has gone through extraordinary changes in age, income, and household make-up. The middle class and traditional American family have literally vanished.

The new customers of the 1990s have many faces; they are markedly different and more diversified than those of the 1970s. Demographers call this the "slicing of America." These smaller, distinct customer groups are what make the marketer's job much more difficult and increases the need for a "monomaniacal obsession" with knowing customers.

THE CHANGING RETAILER

In response to changing consumers, the retail market has started a visible and loud revolution. Main Street retailers have had to define and redefine their business identity and marketing direction as new retailers stake their claim in the marketplace.

In the early 1980s, there were a few factory outlet malls—today there are more than 400. In the early 1980s, Price Club was testing the concept of a "warehouse/wholesale club"—today regional or national "clubs" are in every primary and secondary market. In the early 1980s, Toys R Us was the only significant, national "category killer"—today, almost every retail sector has a monster competitor selling a narrow assortment of goods. In the early 1980s, Wal-Mart had 200 stores in small towns and Kmart was the discount king—today, Wal-Mart is larger than Kmart and Sears combined. In the early 1980s, Sears was the catalog leader—today, there are 8,000 specialty catalogs and Sears is out of the catalog business.

These changes have dramatically affected how the Main Street retailers operate. They must change their merchandising tactics and embrace the concept of "narrowcasting." No longer can the retailer offer adequate service, okay pricing, and "kinda" know their customer. *One Stop Marketing* will show you how to narrow your product assortment, "Nordstromize" your service, and increase the value of your products and services. That is the "how to" component. Whether it's a simple postcard promotion or segmenting your customers, I give you step-by-step suggestions for many "how-to" opportunities.

CORE CUSTOMER

Even though the consumer has been fragmented into many smaller customer groups, every retailer has a core customer. That core customer is the heart of the business. The core customer represents a disproportionately large share of the store sales. They buy similar products. Many of their friends are potential core customers and they respond to the same marketing tactics.

The central thesis of this book is that knowing the core customer is everything in marketing and *One Stop Marketing* shows you how to find and keep your core customer. You'll learn how to promote to your core customer, how to build a promotional plan, and simple tactics to keep your core customers happy long after the sale. You will do this without three consultants and advertising agencies.

THE TWELVE RETAIL MARKETING PRINCIPLES THAT WORK

These marketing principles create the framework. They all work together. They let the retailer see how the customer should and does ultimately form the company. These principles are the result of 20 years marketing experience in retail, manufacturing, and franchising, eight years of teaching marketing and marketing related classes at the college level, and counseling more than 1,400 small business owners.

The twelve marketing principles are not figments of academic imagination. These principles work. In the business world, principles that work are better than principles that are right.

THE WORK OF MARKETING IS FUN

This book is work. Marketing success comes partly from luck, feel, discipline, and analysis. The "Getting Down to Business" sections, which follow each marketing principle, allow you to think about how you will apply the ideas to your store.

Smart marketing is a process that starts and ends with customers. This book follows the process of finding and keeping customers. If you follow the step-by-step approach to finding and keeping customers, the work of marketing will become easy.

Have fun. Your customers will appreciate your smart marketing.

I

MARKETING

1

THE QUIET REVOLUTION: THE CHANGING CUSTOMER

Remember the common phrase of the go-go days of the 1960s and 1970s?: "Invent a better mousetrap and the world will beat a path to your door."

In the 1990s, this is simply not so. The history of business is littered with great products unsold because of mediocre or nonexistent marketing. Whether the product be yogurt, tanning salons, Cajun cooking, or carpeting, the old math, "Throw it against the wall and something will stick," will get you zilch.

The new math of business starts with marketing. The reason is basic. We are in a highly competitive and fragmented market, so successful companies will differentiate their products or stores the way their key customers would want. That is the new mindset, grounded in the real wisdom of marketing—customers, customers, and customers. If I know my customer better than you, I win!

But the customers of the 1960s and the 1970s are not the customers of the 1990s. In 1966, it was easy to direct marketing toward broad middle-class America, the great "nuclear family," where dad worked and mom stayed at home with a couple of ungrateful children. The family aspired to a station wagon and a bigger home. The children played baseball and football; few knew soccer. Mother did the shopping and dad decided when to spend the real money. Mother waited at home all day for the Sears truck finally to deliver a washer. Dad could not find anything in the kitchen. They were the traditional American family.

Not anymore.

3

FRAGMENTED MARKET

We are now experiencing a quiet social revolution—a 10 on the Richter scale of social upheaval—but it is difficult to see and understand the extraordinary changes in age, income, and household composition in our society. This revolution will intensify as we enter the twenty-first century.

Figure 1-1 shows that the traditional American family of the 1960s has virtually vanished. What has replaced the traditional family? Look at Figure 1-2. The nontraditional is now traditional and yesterday's traditional is now nontraditional.

Demographers call this trend the "slicing of America." There is no broad, easily defined middle group for taste, values, and consumption. This is what creates the need for marketing—and makes the marketer's job much harder.

You must learn to identify these smaller groups and everything about them if you are to succeed.

WOMEN IN THE WORKFORCE

A key part of the changing household is women's increased participation in the workforce. Figure 1-3 clearly shows the dramatic change that has taken place in the last 25–30 years.

Much has been written about the effects in society of more women in the workforce. Perhaps the following examples will make the point.

In 1987, the fashion industry decided that short skirts were the new style—but women refused to buy them. Many of these older baby boomers had enjoyed miniskirts when they were teenagers, so it was understandable that the fashion industry would cycle around and offer this look again 20 years later.

These women, though, had changed. They now had careers and families. Many were mothers, 40% had attended college, and 75% were working. Being practical was far more important than being fashionable. One perturbed working woman, Barbara Siegmen, mayor of Princeton, New Jersey, said it all: "Could Lee Iacocca have bailed out Chrysler wearing short pants?"

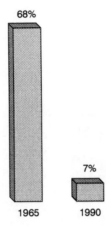

Figure 1-1. Percent of American households that are traditional. (Source: Current Population Survey, Bureau of Census.)

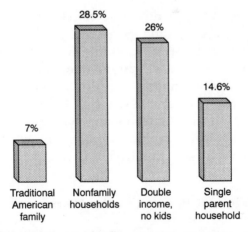

Figure 1-2. Makeup of new American households 1990. (Source: Current Population Survey, Bureau of Census.)

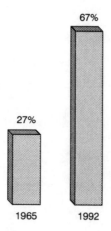

Figure 1-3. Change in women's participation in workforce. (Source: Employment and Earnings, Bureau of Labor Statistics.)

For over 10 years, Sears has felt the sting of the working woman's rejection of Sears' apparel. In September 1993, Sears started a $30 million advertising campaign directed at middle-income working women, with the slogan, "Come see the softer side of Sears."

"Women for the last dozen years have been turned off by Sears, turned off because the stores did not look good and the merchandise was just not the kind that women like to see," said retail consultant Kurt Barnard, president of New York–based Barnard's Retail Marketing Report.

"I mean, what woman really wants to buy a Sears Roebuck cocktail dress? Isn't that somehow an oxymoron?" he said.

Time will tell if the working woman will get the same glow from Sears clothes as she does from a DieHard battery.

A Personal View of Women in the Workforce

In the 1960s and 1970s, the Trivers family resembled the typical American family. Well almost. We had five children.

In 1978, Karen Trivers decided to work outside the home and she was very successful. One year she received a bonus large enough to buy something she had long wanted: a yellow VW Bug convertible. It was not necessarily a practical car for a family of seven, but more a reward for her hard work.

Karen visited a VW dealership in Southern California and brought along Nathan, who was then three years old. When the salesman asked what she was interested in, Karen pointed to the yellow VW Bug convertible and said, "That's the car I want." The salesman said, "Why don't you come back tonight with your husband and we'll discuss prices?" Although Nathan cannot confirm the wording, Karen Trivers told the salesman what she thought about his comment and left.

She stopped at the next dealership she saw, Toyota, where she said to the salesman, "I want to buy that car at that sticker price. I want no hassles and I want it in thirty minutes." The salesman said, "Of course, be happy to help you." Karen drove out with her new car exactly 30 minutes later.

The VW salesman was convinced that Karen was shopping but had neither the money nor the decision-making power to buy. Wrong! And the Toyota salesman? He has been put in the Toyota Hall of Fame for having sold and delivered a brand new car at full sticker price in 30 minutes.

CONVENIENCE QUOTIENT

Due to social changes, the biggest benefit most Americans seek in the 1990s is convenience. Look again at Figure 1-2. To the three largest household types, time is their most precious commodity.

In the 1960s the Leave It to Beaver *family spent time to save money; today, the three largest household types spend money to save time.*

Consider how various retailers and service businesses have raised the convenience quotient by making house calls:

Decorator service	Yard service
Floor covering	House-sitting
Housekeeping	Errand service

Blinds cleaning	Bicycle repair
Auto repair	Gourmet dinner service
Shoe repair	Dog-sitting
Mower repair	Car rental

Also, consider how other services have improved their convenience quotient.

1. *Banking:* Open Saturdays and 24-hour ATMs; ATMs at 185,000 nonbanking locations
2. *Autos:* 10-minute lube, 30-minute tune-ups, instant credit approval for auto purchase, car wash/lube completed in the parking lot
3. *Supermarkets:* Open 24 hours with many separate specialty departments, such as bakery, florist, video rental, delis with take-home dinners, pharmacy, Chinese takeout, banking service, and espresso bar
4. *General retail:* Deliver product within two hours of specified time, open Sundays, open late on weekdays, personal shopper, accept most credit cards
5. *1-800:* 8,000 specialty catalogs, call 24 hours
6. *Gas stations:* Pump and pay at same machine
7. *TV:* Shop at home with TV
8. *Computer:* Shop at home on Internet
9. *Delivery service:* Overnight delivery of letters and packages, fax
10. *Medical:* Immediate-care clinic
11. *Car insurance:* Replace windshield at home
12. *One-hour service:* Photo, shoe repair, eyeglasses, cleaners, suit alterations

We take these conveniences for granted, yet our appetite for more convenience for all products and services has not been sated.

Convenience must be a dominant theme for the Main Street retailer.

THE SQUARING OF THE PYRAMID

For 150 years, regardless of the mortality rate, the makeup of the American population was like a pyramid (Figure 1-4): many younger people, slowly decreasing to very few of the oldest. This has been true regardless of whether old age was considered to be 47 (the average age of death in 1870) or 75. The age pyramid was constant.

Consequently, products, clothes, advertising, education, employment opportunities, and Social Security were all designed for the young. The pyramid was a truism.

Not anymore.

Today, the pyramid is squaring. According to the U.S. Census, in 1993, the number of people over 65 exceeded the number of teenagers and the over-65 group is the fastest-growing age group in the United States. This suggests that some time early in the next century there will be an equal number of people in every five-year group from age one to 70. Figure 1-5 shows how the population will be segmented.

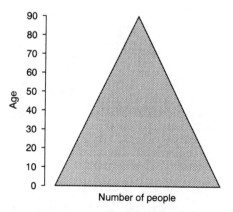

Figure 1-4. The age/population pyramid 1960.

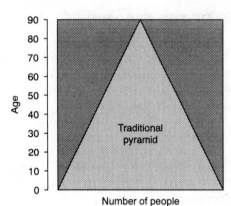

Figure 1-5. The squaring of the age/population pyramid 2010. (Source: Projection of Population of U.S., Bureau of Census.)

Our more important concern is the growth of age groups in the 1990s. Figures 1-6 and 1-7 clearly show from what groups the growth in potential customers will come.

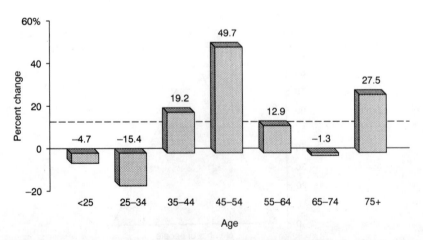

Figure 1-6. Age change, head of household 1990–2000 (%). (Source: Projections of Households and Families, 1990–2000, Bureau of Census.)

Age	<25	25–34	35–44	45–54	55–64	65–74	75+
1990	4.7	21.2	21.1	14.4	12.3	11.7	8.7
2000	4.4	18.0	25.3	21.6	13.9	11.6	11.1

Figure 1-7. Age change, head of household 1990–2000 (millions). (Source: Projections of Households and Families, 1990–2000, Bureau of Census.)

Consider how the squaring of the pyramid is reflected in today's consumer marketing.

A. Senior citizens (over 65) have money and power. *Modern Maturity,* the magazine for members of the American Association of Retired Persons, has twice the readership of *People*. Seniors receive special treatment and discounts from restaurants, banks, retailers, public transportation, and even universities. They pay cash, thank you. Many won't buy on credit.

B. Older Americans (55–64) wear underwear, dresses, slacks, and swimsuits, and they want to see happy, healthy, older models in their image—not svelte teenagers. Older Americans love to travel to faraway places and buy the "better or best" products.

C. Older baby boomers (45–54) are credit card–crazed consumers—they love the feel of plastic. This affluent group has created tremendous growth in catalogs, but they have single-handedly rejected general catalogs like Sears and Montgomery Ward. Give them Spiegel or give them death.

A PERSONAL VIEW OF SENIORS

One morning Karen Trivers was waiting in a doughnut shop in Grants Pass, Oregon. A young construction worker stood in front of her. Both were listening to three seniors reminiscing about the "good old days."

"But when I think of dancers, nobody could match Fred Astaire and Ginger Rogers." Agreement again, "Yes, they were something."

"Hey, but I've got one for you guys. Edgar Bergen and Charlie McCarthy. They could make me laugh 'til I cried." They all smiled, "What good fun."

Karen recognized the names of these famous old entertainers, but the young construction worker had a quizzical look on his face. Karen asked, "Do you know who they're talking about?" "No, I sure don't," he replied, "I'm new to this area. I'm from Idaho."

There is a lot of Idaho in all of us.

BRAINY . . . BUT CONFUSED

Today's consumers are better educated than their parents. However, they are product ignorant. This is not a contradiction. Many consumers today are confused about products and their claims of greatness. However, the confusion is a measure of an intensely competitive environment, not the consumer's I.Q. Today's consumer wants to learn about the product. "Trust me" won't sell.

Far too many Main Street retailers have ill-trained salespeople who fill time and/or space. Their knowledge of products is weak and the displays and store signage are not much better. It's no wonder that customers turn to catalogs for informed salespeople and intelligent presentations, even if they are 2,000 miles away.

The retail store that succeeds in the 1990s is one that does not play the customer for an idiot, but respects the customer and gives the customer the information needed to make an informed decision. However, the information must be delivered in the customer's terms, not industry lingo.

Conclusion

In the 1960s and 1970s, there was a clear mass market that represented an enormous buying force, and its members were very similar in their tastes, values, and consumption habits. There is no similar in their tastes, values, and consumption habits. There is no mass market today. Instead, there are many smaller markets that have different social behavior and consumption habits.

In the 1960s, when a 35-year-old woman went shopping, her demographics and shopping habits were clear. She was paired to her first husband, had three children, went shopping for children's clothes and food for the household. She looked at, but did not buy, big-ticket items.

In the 1990s, she's more likely to be the single head of the household than married to her first husband. If she is married, she's likely not to have children. If she has children, she could be a stepmother to her husband's children, and on and on. When a 35-year-old woman goes shopping, it's anyone's guess what she will buy: baby clothes, running shoes, flowers for a friend, off-white wedding gown, college textbooks, briefcase, airline tickets for a business meeting, or a lawyer to get rid of a lout.

The successful Main Street retailer must know the distinct markets (groups of people) that buy from their store. The act of defining markets and then creating specific benefits for those markets is called "segmenting" and "targeting," and it is at the heart of successful marketing for the 1990s.

2

THE LOUD REVOLUTION: THE CHANGING RETAILER

In response to the quiet social revolution taking place in the United States, the retail market started a very visible and loud revolution which continues today and has gained intensity. Main Street retailers have had to define and redefine their business identity and marketing direction as general merchandisers flail about and new retailers stake their claim in the marketplace.

Older retailers who have failed to adjust to the slicing of America have vanished. Some are confused but still around. Others have changed and are flourishing. But this loud revolution is really about the many forms of new retail competition that have come on the scene:

"Take No Prisoners"
Home Depot, Circuit City, Incredible Universe, Toys-"R"-Us, OfficeMax, Barnes & Noble, Virgin Records, and 30 other superstores or category killers

"Price, Price, Price"
Wal-Mart, Price Club, Costco Wholesale Club, Sam's Club

"Panic, We're Drowning"
Sears, Montgomery Ward, and most department stores

"Perception, Maybe, Not Reality"
400 factory outlet malls

"Call 1-800, Sip Wine, and Use My Credit Card"
Spiegel, L.L. Bean, Lands' End, Victoria's Secret, and 8,000 other oversaturated, overpromised, direct-marketing companies

"Great and Not So Great National Franchises"
Wicks 'N' Sticks, Benetton, H & R Block, Roto Rooter, and 1,200 others offering the American dream

TRIVERS RETAIL METER

There are so many new and diverse forms of retail competition that Main Street retailers feel hopelessly outgunned. They should not.

In the spring and fall of 1994, I shopped at least four stores in each category I have listed. I evaluated each store for pricing, stock availability, helpfulness of store personnel, after-sale customer service, and promotions and advertising.

Make no mistake: Each new type of competition provided dramatic, new opportunities for their targeted customer, but each store had glaring weaknesses. Take heart: No business is perfect. Big is often ugly, and it is your job to capitalize on their ugliness, to be pretty where they are ugly, to be strong where they are weak, and to crow to the heavens about the difference.

TAKE NO PRISONERS

Home Depot, OfficeMax, et al.

Strengths
- Dominant retailer in their niche
- Massive assortment
- Appearance of massive inventory
- Appearance of low price on every item

Weaknesses
- Out of stock on advertised items
- Poor store service
- Little after-sale service
- Many products are not the lowest price in town

These retailers are the most dominant in their market niche, with at least five times the retail space of the independent retailer, an incredible assortment of merchandise, and what appears to be massive inventories. If the Main Street retailer has six varieties of something, Home Depot will have 60, and so on.

Most of the big retailers attempt to give service they feel is equal to or better than their Main Street competition. Circuit City's slogan is, "Where service is state of the art." Home Depot spends substantial time on product training for salespeople. In reality, the ratio of customers to employees is so high that the customer service sometimes is no more than "quick McAnswers," and not at all personable. And what are your chances of finding the same person next time? In my experience, it's not very good. These stores do not deliver believable, sustainable, in-store service and they absolutely flunk after-sale service.

As you can see from my retail meter in Figure 2-1, I have rated their pricing as a comparative strength and weakness. On

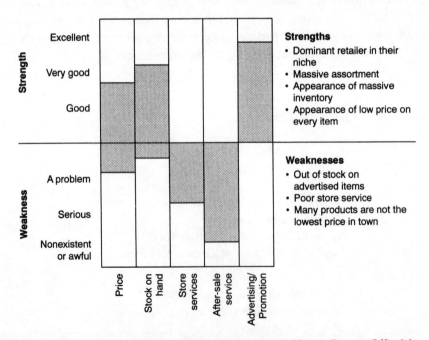

Figure 2-1. Trivers retail meter—take no prisoners, Home Depot, OfficeMax, et al.

their key promotional items (about 25% of all "on sale" products) and their key everyday high unit (sale) producers (about 18% of all items in the store) the pricing is excellent—equal to or lower than the lowest price in town. But the rest of their products are priced equal to Main Street retailers. Main Street retailers should consider that a weakness.

The same double rating applies to their stock on hand. They have committed to a very large inventory investment, but with constant advertising, price reductions on many items, and a wide selection of brands that do their own advertising (GE, IBM, Sony, etc.), they have an extremely difficult time keeping a balanced inventory. An executive with one of these companies told me the stock for 35% of their promotional items runs out before the promotion ends! Do not minimize this weakness. Rain checks do not create customer goodwill. A society that values convenience loathes the inconvenience of not being able to buy when they are ready.

"Take no prisoners" businesses will massively out-advertise the independent retailer. When they advertise, they create product interest and demand for their store and any store that carries the same product.

Ride along with their advertising and have special, in-store signage declaring, "The price of the depot, the service of professionals." Do not try to outmuscle their advertising. It would be business suicide.

PRICE, PRICE, PRICE

Price Club, Sam's Club, et al.

Strength
- □ Low price

Weaknesses
- □ Concrete slab floor
- □ Must buy very large quantity size
- □ Don't carry same item all the time
- □ No service. Period!

Discounters abound. For many years Kmart was the sole national discounter. Now Wal-Mart is the general merchandise discounter, with the consistently lowest price. In markets where Kmart was established and Wal-Mart arrived as the new kid on the block, Wal-Mart would inflict a 10% to 15% sales decrease on the older retailer and Kmart would lose its position as the town's key discounter.

Clubs are the newest breed of discounters. Their prices are stunningly low, clearly lower than either "Mart," but the quantity you have to purchase and the shopping environment are major weaknesses. Who needs 250 feet of plastic wrap or 20 pounds of pistachios? More people than one would think.

The clubs have no frills. Concrete floors, industrial shelving, and a simple marketing program, "Stack it high, and watch it fly." They can't even spell customer service, and the check-out process is akin to leaving prison—trust is not part of their program.

I have not rated advertising for these retailers in Figure 2-2. Generally speaking, they do very little advertising. That may be considered a weakness, but the power of their "price" identity precludes them from substantial advertising. They say, "If we advertise, our prices must go up."

With the proliferation of clubs and superstores, "We've got the lowest price," is promised every day by a different retailer. "Guaranteed lowest price" is a phrase used so often that it would seem possible to buy a name-brand TV and, if you were willing to go from store to store demanding the lowest price, you would finally find a store that would give you the TV for free, and would also give you $10 to go away.

But the issue of price for the Main Street retailer is no laughing matter. Today, consumers' price consciousness is very high. The clubs did not create this price consciousness; the consumer did.

I don't pretend to know all the factors that caused this resurgence of discount shopping, but the following are fundamental contributions:

☐   Middle-class wage earners are earning less today than they were 10 years ago.

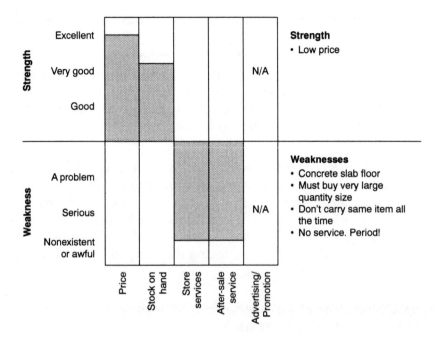

Figure 2-2. Trivers retail meter—price, price, price, Price Club, Sam's Club, et al.

☐ Corporate layoffs or downsizing are directly affecting middle-class wage earners. More than one million mid-level employees of big corporations have been terminated in the last five years and they are not finding jobs of equal pay.

☐ The mid-level terminations have sent shock waves through all wage earners. Those jobs were sacrosanct, and people in those positions were on the way up, not out. Even in the era of greed, many Americans started to become frugal, either out of necessity or fear.

☐ Many major manufacturers had created brand value by selectively distributing their brands to limited numbers or types of retailers. To increase sales, they began selling their brand to direct-marketing companies (catalogs), Sears, Kmart, and specialty chains. Suddenly, Calvin Klein and many other brands could be found almost everywhere, and retailers started using price to move the goods. Why buy Calvin Klein at department-store price when the same item can be purchased for less elsewhere?

☐ New technologies, combined with new ways of doing business, have allowed many new companies such as Southwest Airlines, Wal-Mart, etc., to reduce cost dramatically and pass the savings on to the customer.

For the Main Street retailer, the issue is not why, but how? How will this change in consumer buying affect my business? How can service offset the customer's concern for buying at the lowest price? How do I increase the value of the product and the value of buying from my store to justify my price, which is not the lowest? (We will discuss these questions and others about outfoxing the competition later in Section IV, Keeping Customers.)

PANIC, WE'RE DROWNING

Sears, department stores, et al.

Strengths
- ☐ Name recognition
- ☐ Credit
- ☐ Customer satisfaction
- ☐ Heavy advertiser

Weaknesses
- ☐ Overinflated prices
- ☐ In-store service
- ☐ Out of stock of advertised items
- ☐ Must fight for customer satisfaction

This group does not include Nordstrom—the fabulously successful department store that started in Seattle and is now opening stores in the East. It is known for fabled customer service and is the envy of all other department stores. This group is about the envious.

Knowing where to shop used to be so simple. The department store customer bought clothes at the department store and a washer or dryer from Sears. When the regular Sears customers hit their credit limit with Sears, they would buy from Montgomery Ward and, if the neighbors were not watching, go to Kmart. These were symbiotic relationships. Not anymore.

The best department store customer today is probably the best Target customer and loves the factory outlet malls. You will not find this same customer at Wal-Mart, but you can bet you'll see her in Costco, Home Depot, and Circuit City on the weekends.

The reason I have included department stores and Sears/Ward dinosaurs in my retail review is that they can and have created tremendous confusion as they try to figure out how to compete against the new competition. They are not taking rejection very well!

All these older businesses conduct market research on a regular basis so it is not surprising that in early 1991 they discovered their customers did not like the marketing programs using the "high regular price to justify the reduced advertised price." The customer considered the regular price fake and the reduced price the regular price. Certainly sales showed that most customers waited for the sale or bought elsewhere if the item was not on sale.

Within six months of each other, Sears and Ward marketed "everyday low prices," reduced their advertising budget, and promptly had a sales decrease. After 100 years of off-price advertising and overinflated regular prices, Sears and Ward could not convince their core customers that they had changed. Customers waited for the promotions and when they didn't occur, they went elsewhere. These retailers advertise heavily today, but their regular price for most goods is more than that of most Main Street retailers. They are easy competition on price.

Due to their high sales of advertised items and constant changing of advertised items, they experience an unacceptable out of stock condition. Rain checks are inconvenient and a major weakness.

A clerk that can be found is probably a part-timer and a floater who worked in bras yesterday and is selling tires today. If you need a manager to get approval, forget it.

On every door to a Sears store is its motto, "Satisfaction guaranteed or your money back." Sears and Ward started as catalog businesses and that assurance of customer satisfaction helped build their respective catalog markets. Satisfaction guaranteed is part of Sears' culture in both retail and catalog. A store manager can be fired if the corporate office receives too many customer complaints. That's why I rated the after-sale service good in Figure 2-3, but it's also a weakness. How long does it take to resolve a complaint or get a defective product replaced? How many layers of store management need to review the initial decision? Delayed satisfaction is inconvenient and frustrating. You will get what you want, but by the time you get it, you will feel no level of satisfaction and will tell your friends of the frustration of dealing with an uncaring bureaucracy.

These old companies cannot Nordstromize their service. It's in the genes.

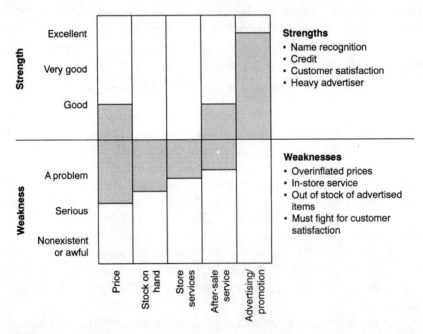

Figure 2-3. Trivers retail meter—panic, we're drowning, Sears, department stores, et al.

PERCEPTION, MAYBE, NOT REALITY

Factory outlet stores

Strengths
- ☐ Real savings on old, dropped, irregular, and poor-selling merchandise
- ☐ Mall setting—great variety of product

Weaknesses
- ☐ Regular running line, no savings to customer
- ☐ No continuity of product offering
- ☐ No advertising

About 20 years ago, L.L. Bean, the catalog company, invented the idea of the factory outlet mall as we know it today. L.L. Bean and all catalog companies have a unique problem: how to liquidate old, dropped, shopworn merchandise or misbuys. Since its catalog is its store and it is not a good place to dump product, L.L. Bean established a liquidation store next to its factory in Freeport, Maine.

This was truly a factory outlet store. Millions came to Maine from Boston and New York City to save—and save they did! All the merchandise was distressed; none was running line.

The customer who drove six hours to save was the young, department store customer, the early yuppie. Manufacturers soon realized that these urban shoppers could be found on weekends in this small town in Maine, and they all had a "save" sign stamped on their forehead, a smile on their lips, and plastic in their hands. So better-known department-store brands (American Tourister, Canon Mills, Ralph Lauren, London Fog, etc.) opened their own factory outlet stores for distressed goods close to the L.L. Bean store. Almost overnight the entire downtown of Freeport became a factory outlet mall. It was a fabulous success.

Today, with more than 400 copycats around the country, the outlet mall idea has been adulterated. The outlet stores are selling distressed goods and attempting to sell first-quality, running-line (active line merchandise) goods at prices that will not undercut their regular customers (department and specialty stores). I recently purchased some running-line luggage from one of these stores and the clerk assured me that if Weinstock's (a local department store) had the item on sale for less, this store would refund the difference, within 30 days of purchase. Sure enough, Weinstock's did and I returned to the outlet for a refund. "Did you bring the ad?" "No." "You'll need the ad for a refund." And so it went. I finally received my refund (mailed to me from corporate headquarters four weeks later). I learned my lesson. Distressed goods, yes. Running-line goods, no!

You can see why I've rated pricing both a strength and weakness in Figure 2-4.

Outlet stores typically do not advertise, as a commitment to their regular customers (department and specialty stores). They

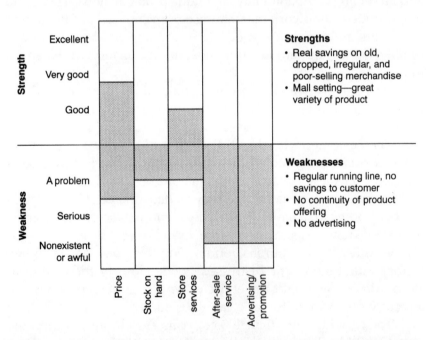

Figure 2-4. Trivers retail meter—perception, maybe, not reality, factory outlet stores.

also do not have consistent product offering. They sell what the company wants to get rid of, not what the customer is looking to buy.

I believe the factory outlet malls are losing their luster. They have compromised their basic reason for being and no longer are what they were intended to be.

CALL 1-800, SIP WINE, AND USE MY CREDIT CARD

Spiegel, Lands' End, et al.

Strengths
- □ Convenience
- □ Great variety and dominance
- □ Customer service
- □ After-sale service

Weaknesses
- □ Can't see and feel goods
- □ Delivery time
- □ Return hassle

Main Street retailers know that the catalog retailers or direct-marketing companies have a built-in advantage. Lands' End does not have to charge the customer a state sales tax; the Main Street retailer must. But that is just a small factor in the incredible growth of this new form of competition.

This industry was dominated by Sears and Montgomery Ward for 75 years. Today, neither is in the catalog business but 8,000 small specialty catalogs have enjoyed tremendous success. For the past 10 years, direct marketing has grown at twice the rate of conventional retail. The key benefit to the consumer is not saving the sales tax or lower prices, it is convenience. The growth is coming from metropolitan areas, fueled by harried, double-income families.

It's worthwhile to take a closer look at this new competition. Direct marketing (direct mail, catalogs, telemarketing, TV) is a microcosm of the changing face of the American consumer and the principles of modern marketing that best attract this fragmented society.

Even with the tax savings, the price of products in catalogs is a weakness. By and large, products from catalogs are higher than Main Street retail, and you have to wait five to seven days to receive the goods. Certain customer groups, like older senior citizens, do not trust direct marketing and about 30% of the entire population won't buy anything they can't touch or see (Figure 2–5).

Why, then, does this competition do so well? Why does it outperform Main Street retail?

Direct marketing has capitalized on the slicing of America by offering narrow assortments of products (narrowcasting) to a narrow group of customers. They know their customer better than the Main Street retailer or any of the other forms of new competition. Direct marketing gets an A^+ on the four key tactics of modern marketing: knowing your customer, convenience, dominance, and service. But you don't have to be in the catalog business to get an A^+. I will show you how.

The direct marketer calls "knowing your customer" database management. The direct marketer knows each customer by name, their address, what the customer purchased, how they paid for it, what size and color, and from which specific catalog it was chosen. The direct marketer knows how often the customer made a purchase from the company and whether the product was returned or a complaint lodged. All this can and must be part of the Main Street retailer's marketing program. All it takes is a computer.

Certainly it is inconvenient to wait a week for your purchase, but it is so convenient to order: Call 1-800 (it's free), anytime (not 9 to 5), hassle free (at home, kids in bed), with the miracle of plastic. It's like getting a gift for yourself, and only you and the UPS driver know.

I'm not suggesting that you get into the catalog business, but conventional retailers must be sure that their operation is very convenient for their customers.

The idea of narrowcasting and dominance is everywhere. Look at the media. For 30 years, TV was ABC, NBC, and CBS. They were like Sears and Montgomery Ward, offering a little bit of everything to the public. Cable TV emerged and the big three laughed. "Who

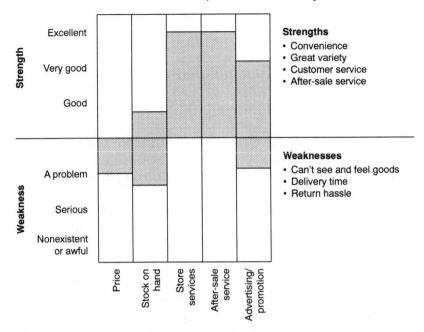

Figure 2-5. Trivers retail meter—call 1-800 . . . , Spiegel, Land's End, et al.

is going to watch one channel that just has sports (ESPN) or news (CNN) or, what a joke, weather (Weather Channel)?'' Who indeed!

Look at magazines. Thirty years ago, this industry was dominated by their own Sears and Ward—*Look* and *Life*. When *Sports Illustrated* launched their magazine directed just at sports, the venerable giants had a good laugh. The giants are gone and though *Sports Illustrated* has flourished, there now are more than 140 magazines directed at specific sports and very narrow sports topics: weight lifting, power lifting, and making your thigh muscle your friend (I made that up).

TV, magazines, radio, repair services, doctors, retail, lawyers, you name it, they are all practicing narrowcasting. The good ones do a few things very well and are dominant in their narrow market. The Main Street retailer can no longer offer a little bit of many different things (this is called delicatessen marketing), but must focus on marketing a *larger assortment of fewer products.* Narrowcasting works because customers want it. They want to watch the shows, read the magazines, and shop at stores that interest them and satisfy their needs.

Narrowcasting is the marketer's response to the slicing of America.

It seems incredible, but most catalog customers believe that they get better service from someone they can't see than from their Main Street retailer. The catalog company employee is more personal, friendly, efficient, and knowledgeable while taking an order and even when resolving a complaint. And the guarantee of complete customer satisfaction from these companies is akin to unconditional love. The customer is right, period.

These companies have exploited a weakness of the Main Street retailer. Far too often, employees fill space and time, with little or no training and not much interest in customers. It ain't pretty, but it's true.

However, for most direct-marketing consultants, the bloom is off the rose for their beloved industry. The good news for the Main Street retailer is that the direct-marketing industry is now in the mature stage, with a tremendous overcapacity of catalogs and products. For the rest of the 1990s, they will experience single-digit sales increases, and half of the companies will vanish. Competitive cannibalism. As sales slow down and margins decrease, service will begin to deteriorate, returns will become a bigger hassle, and liquidation of distressed goods will be more costly.

If the Main Street retailer commits to narrowcasting, dominant presentations, inventory of fewer items, trained salespeople, and convenience, customers can begin to be pulled away from catalog companies.

GREAT AND NOT-SO-GREAT NATIONAL FRANCHISES

Wicks 'N' Sticks, Benetton, et al.

Franchising has become a major factor in the retail and service industries. Today, 40% of all retail sales in the United States come from franchises. It would be presumptuous to use the Trivers retail meter for 1,200 diverse franchises, so, instead, I will offer some observations about this form of competition.

Generally, the benefits to the consumer of buying from franchises are consistent quality, similar merchandise, identical display and store layout, same pricing policy, and implicit "franchisor friend" if something goes wrong.

The benefits are a double-edged sword. Many customers find that the similarity of product and display reduces the incentive to buy from the franchise retailer if they are visiting another town. If you've seen one Wicks 'N' Sticks, you've seen them all.

Since franchises are part of a national group, most do not offer products unique to the specific customers in the different markets they serve. Cookie-cutter marketing has serious drawbacks: It targets the statistical average customer who bought the statistical average best-seller in the statistical average town. For fast food that might be okay, but for many products and services, that is a recipe for disaster.

Like any competition, each franchise does some things that are worth copying. (Remember, plagiarism is an important part of the marketing process. Be sure to copy the good and let them keep the bad.) Pay close attention to new and different displays and products. New store warranties (not product-, but store-related) and new, take-home point-of-purchase material generally signify a change of marketing direction. In most cases, the new direction is based on pretty sophisticated national market research. (It's always helpful to have your competition do your research for you. Just don't thank them.)

Conclusion

The Main Street retailer must convince the customer that their store has exactly what the customer wants. That is precisely what your competition is doing. When you define yourself and tell the customer what you do best, you imply that your competition is not doing what you do, or at least, not doing it as well. Think of Avis and its "We try harder" slogan. It gave Avis credit for a "can-do" attitude. The slogan also implied Hertz was lazy and took customers for granted.

I suggest the following approach to defining your Main Street retail business:

- ☐ Become the Avis of a narrow business segment. Capitalize on the big chains' weaknesses. Don't go toe-to-toe with the competition on their customer-perceived strengths.
- ☐ Watch what the competition does, not what they say. When they don't keep their promise, go after them. Tell the world.
- ☐ Never be overserviced. Many of your competitors are making claims of "lowest price" and "never being undersold." Stay away from that constant diet and promise "never to be overserviced." Then you must back it up!
- ☐ Nordstromize your service. Salespeople must be trained, retrained, and trained again. Never stop training. "We're a family business and we're nice," won't do it. Train on every aspect of the business—product, phone skills, helping the customer, and after-sale service.
- ☐ Act direct. Be direct. Don't enter the direct-marketing or catalog business, but do imitate their marketing tactics. It takes a computer and commitment.
- ☐ Narrowcast or expand. Fit or fat. Don't get caught in the middle with delicatessen marketing—where you offer a little bit of a lot of items. Have greater variety of fewer items, or more items and increased inventory investment. As the saying goes, "The choice is yours"—but you must make a choice.

3

THE SMART
MARKETING DEFINITION

**Marketing is the process of finding and then
keeping customers.**

There are many textbook definitions of marketing, but that,
from Theodore Levitt, hits the mark.

Ray Considine, a noted retail consultant, uses the "customer
loyalty ladder" (Figure 3-1) to illustrate this significant point.

Most retailers follow conventional (traditional) advertising to
find customers. When you advertise in a newspaper, anybody who
reads the newspaper is a "suspect." Those who are not interested
in your product ignore your ad. Those who pay some attention
are "prospects." Fewer people actually respond and come to your
store and buy. Those who do come and buy are "customers."
Unfortunately, most retailers follow the process repeatedly: running ads, directed at all the suspects, hoping that a few will become customers.

A great marketing company (Figure 3-2) knows that only half
the job is done when the prospect becomes a customer. A great
marketing company tries to advance the customer up the loyalty
ladder to become a "client," a customer who buys a second time
and potentially becomes an "advocate," a customer who gives
unpaid advertising for the store products and services.

A great marketing company believes that the customer is their
most important "asset"—more important than inventory, the

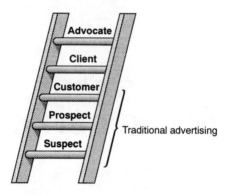

Figure 3-1. Customer loyalty ladder.

building, trucks, and everything a retailer owns. The customer, unlike the truck, can and will find new customers for your store.

It takes at least three times as much money to attract a new customer via traditional forms of advertising as to re-attract a repeat customer. It takes at least 30 times as much marketing money to attract a new customer via traditional forms of advertising as to have a satisfied customer find new customers for you (Figure 3-3).

Sadly, most retailers spend less than 5% of their marketing dollars on their only real asset (the customer) and frantically spend 95% of their marketing dollars to try to find new customers in the

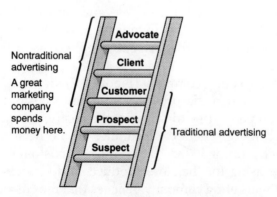

Figure 3-2. How to allocate marketing dollars.

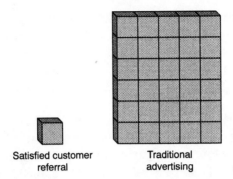

Satisfied customer
referral

Traditional
advertising

Figure 3-3. Value of satisfied customer.

least productive form of communication—traditional advertising (Figure 3-4).

Direct marketers understand, better than anyone else, the loyalty ladder and the need to invest in a satisfied customer. First, they know who their customers are. Second, they know the real marketing secret is that your best customer is your most recent customer. Third, your best word-of-mouth advertising always comes from the most recent customer.

Consider the story of Garden Way, a 15-year-old company that sells rototillers (not exactly a high repeat item). Basically, you buy one tiller in your lifetime. So how do they use the loyalty

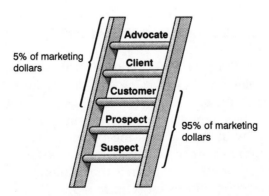

Figure 3-4. Typical retail marketing investment.

ladder? Every month, Garden Way sends out a gardening newspaper which includes surprise gifts, planting charts, service charts, bulletins, factory service tips, courses in gardening . . . and it never asks for an order. Every month, 25% of its sales come directly from word-of-mouth advertising by satisfied customers who are Garden Way advocates, and proud of it.

Direct marketers know how to engineer repeat business by word of mouth. They view customers differently than most Main Street retailers. How many supermarket managers look at a customer and say, "That person represents $50,000 in future sales: $100 a week for 10 years. She also could and/or should represent an additional $50,000 in sales by telling her friends about our great service." That is looking at the customer in an entirely different way. Sadly, supermarkets do not think in those terms. Supermarkets do not know their core customer. The only way they know to create loyalty is to churn out ads and coupons.

Auto dealers are notorious at forgetting about customers the minute they drive off the lot. The average car dealer spends, along with manufacturers' national advertising support, about $335 to find a customer who buys. What do they spend to keep the customer, to engineer word-of-mouth advertising? A 32-cent stamp and a crummy thank-you card.

Lesson learned: The customer who has purchased products from you is the least expensive marketing way to find new customers. People love to tell if they are happy.

WHAT IF THE CUSTOMER IS UNHAPPY?

You have everything to lose if you don't know about or how to resolve a problem, and everything to gain if you do.

Resolving a problem is not the "problem" for retailers. Knowing that there is a problem or knowing that the customer is not truly satisfied with the store is the problem. The customer who writes a letter is not the problem; the problem is the "nice" customer who is unhappy, doesn't complain to the retailer, but quietly trashes the store to all who will listen (Figure 3-5).

Why are these nice customers unhappy? If you ask a retailer why customers don't return, the retailer blames lower prices from

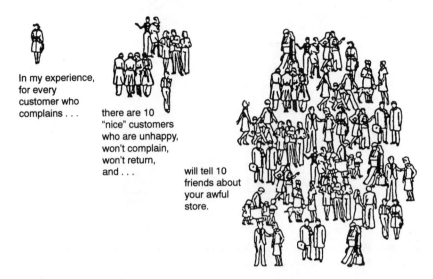

In my experience, for every customer who complains . . .

there are 10 "nice" customers who are unhappy, won't complain, won't return, and . . .

will tell 10 friends about your awful store.

Figure 3-5. The unhappy "nice" customer.

competition or poor quality from the manufacturer. The customer's perception is quite different. When you ask customers the same question, they cite retailer indifference (Figure 3-6). Customers define retailer indifference as:

Untrained salespeople
Out of stock of advertised item
No genuine after-sale service on large purchases
Understaffed
Hard to return purchase
Retailer won't help on manufacturer's product warranty.

YOUR BEST AND WORST CUSTOMER IS YOUR MOST RECENT CUSTOMER

The customer who just purchased from you and liked your store is more apt to repurchase from you than someone who has never

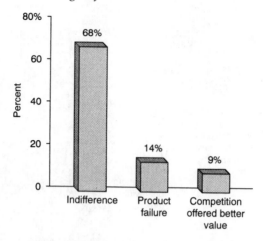

Figure 3-6. Why customers left for the competition. (Source: Betsy Sanders, Fabled Service, Pfeiffer and Co., 1995.)

bought from you or someone who bought from you long ago. Your best word-of-mouth advertising comes from your most recent happy customer.

Your worst customer, who will rip you apart to all their friends, is your most recent unhappy customer.

No matter how you look at it, being in front of your recent customer in a consistent and imaginative way will create goodwill and sales quicker than any other marketing or advertising idea. This is what keeping customers is all about.

BASIC PROGRAM

It is essential to establish a basic program to create goodwill from satisfied customers and find those customers who are marginally satisfied or just plain unhappy with your store. It has been my experience that correcting a problem will convert an unhappy customer to an advocate. Willingly correct a problem, and the customer will sing your praises to many people. This does not suggest that you have planned screwups so you can fix them. There are enough unplanned screwups in your business life!

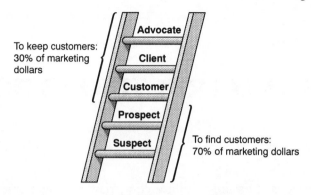

Figure 3-7. How to invest in finding and keeping customers.

Marketing dollars should be spent to reflect this basic definition of marketing: finding and keeping customers. As Figure 3-7 indicates, 30% of your marketing dollars should be spent on keeping customers. Not 5% . . . 30%!

After Section II, Marketing Principles, this book is devoted to retail programs to help you find and then keep customers. The necessary ingredients are discipline and commitment to this simple definition of marketing.

4

WHAT MARKETING IS NOT

1. *Marketing is not selling.* Selling comprises the retailer's need to convert product into cash. A marketer takes cues from the buyer so that the product becomes the consequence of the marketing effort and not vice versa.

2. *Marketing is not industry driven.* "That's the industry standard." "That's how the industry does it." "That's the typical industry guarantee." "Follow the leader." None of that is marketing.

3. *Marketing is not internal-memo driven.* All organizations naturally gravitate inward toward the management. Employees look into the organization for answers. A marketing company looks to the customer for answers and changes the organization.

4. *Marketing is not senior-management-genius driven.* Most business owners believe in their own infallibility. They are, "always right and never in doubt!" Marketing believes the customer is always right. Who cares about the owner?

5. *No Big Bang theory of marketing.* There is no one ad, price, or great promotion that will correct everything. Marketing is commitment and discipline to finding and keeping customers.

5

YOUR MARKETING KNOW-HOW

		Yes	No
1.	Once a month, I sit down with 10 customers who have purchased from me in the last few months and discuss their perception of my business.	___	___
2.	Once a year, I complete some do-it-yourself market research about customers and/or my competition.	___	___
3.	I send a thank-you card to every customer who has spent $100 or more at my business.	___	___
4.	I have a very active customer list.	___	___
5.	I use testimonial ads with satisfied customers.	___	___
6.	My salespeople spend their first four minutes with the customer finding out about the customer and their needs.	___	___
7.	My salespeople talk in customer terms, not industry lingo.	___	___
8.	My products are organized the way the customer would like to buy them.	___	___
9.	I spend 30% of my marketing dollars on keeping customers and 70% on finding customers.	___	___

Score

Each Yes is worth 10 points. Each No is worth 0. If your score is 100, throw this book away and write your own with accompanying video. I'll be the first to order! If your score is less than 100, read on.

II

MARKETING PRINCIPLES

6

THE 12 RETAIL MARKETING PRINCIPLES THAT WORK

The language of marketing is easy to imitate. I have met too many business owners who can "talk the talk" ("focus," "synergy," "target like a rifle shot," "bottom line," and much more) but don't understand the underlying principles or reasons why they should analyze an issue a certain way. Few know how to apply these principles to their small business. It all becomes verbal window dressing, and nothing more.

In Section II, you will learn the key principles of marketing and how different Main Street retailers have applied them, and you will get a chance to apply them to your business. Be sure to complete the Getting Down to Business form at the end of each principle. It gives you the opportunity to improve your retail marketing and look at your business the way your customers do. When you complete these thought-provoking questions, you'll be one of a few Main Street retailers who can walk the walk of marketing.

The central thrust of these principles is that everything a business does should be evaluated from the consumer's point of view.

Know the customer, take the lead from the customer, and you will be one of a kind.

Remember, if you truly embrace the marketing concept, you will construct your own new and better marketing principles for your store.

Trivers' Immutable Law for Marketing Principles
Principles that work are always better than principles
that are right.

MARKETING PRINCIPLE 1

1.

Marketing starts with customers—the marketer works backward from the customer to the product, customer to services, customer to warranty, and customer to sales presentation.

Marketing never starts with products or promotions. Never take a product and make a story for the customer. It is, in fact, the other way around.

Marketing changes made by American Express and JCPenney exemplify successful applications of this principle.

In the early 1970s and 1980s, American Express marketed its credit card toward businessmen: "Don't leave home without it" and "Do you know me?" It was almost accidental that a marketing analyst for the company detected a trend. More women were using their husbands' cards for a variety of uses, and American Express card applications by single women were doubling each year.

In the early 1980s American Express recognized the new buying power and independent decision making of working women. This led to its successful "Part of interesting lives" campaign directed solely at working women. Three groups of working women were targeted: married, single, and single/head of household. Each group was offered different benefits for basically the same product—an American Express credit card.

This is a classic example of working backward from the customer to service offered.

In fall 1993, JCPenney announced that it would pursue more Latino and African-American customers by offering products that appealed especially to them. By studying minority consumer attitudes, buying habits, and products preferred, JCPenney realized that it was not offering these customers what they wanted and was missing some of this $360 billion potential market. In response, Penney offered authentic African and Latino apparel in selected stores, as well as items for bedding, bath, decorative wall coverings, and wall art.

This principle of starting with the customer might sound like an elementary rule of business, but that does not keep it from being violated.

Consider the personal computer industry. Every day there are new technologies and new applications—all from computer specialists and engineers, not customers. Everything comes from a computer genius and is directed at frustrated, intimidated, and very confused customers. This is the nonmarketing, inside/outside approach to the marketplace. Very little, if any, advice or direction flows from the customer (outside) to the computer maker (inside). Marketing in the computer industry is almost nonexistent. The industry leaders said that every home in America would have a personal computer by 1993. Only 32% do, which is not surprising.

In Detroit, the automobile industry spends millions of dollars on marketing research. In fact, that is what market research is all about—thinking backward from the customer. So why didn't Detroit see the trend toward compact cars or the customer's insistence on quality? The answer is that American automakers never really researched the customer's wants; GM and others only researched customer preference among choices offered. In other words, GM asked customers to choose from three car designs it was considering. It did not offer the customer what the customer really wanted, which was none of the three.

View from Main Street

Principle 1 is attitude first, tactic second. It concerns looking at your business from the customer's standpoint, not selectively or when the customer complains, but at all times for all business and personnel decisions.

Jim Stanton of Junction City, Oregon (not his name, he doesn't want to be kidded and fined by his local Rotary club) returned from a business workshop run by the Small Business Development Center at the local community college. It was billed as a marketing workshop, but the whole session centered on the following three questions:

1. If you were to start your business today as a new venture, would it look and behave like your existing store?
2. Do you know your customers as well as you know your suppliers?
3. Are your employees more loyal to your customers than to you?

You can imagine how the retailers responded to those questions: They answered No to all three. Some asked for their money back and left. Jim decided to stay and quickly realized the value of the workshop. He took a closer look and discovered that a marketing company would have answered Yes to those questions. Jim recognized how far his 18-year gift business had strayed from what he initially started. He was not happy.

Jim started his business with little money, less space, but with a big idea and many customer-centered policies. His store slowly changed and evolved, but the changes came from putting out fires, manufacturer representatives' ideas (invariably they only help the manufacturer), media salespeople, employees, and assorted friends. Since the customer was not part of that dialogue, you can bet that Jim's store was different than if he were to start it today.

On the first day of business, Jim knew his customers, sought their advice, told them of his plans, and barely knew his suppliers. A year later, it was just the opposite.

The store never had an "If you broke it, you bought it" sign, but that occasionally was the atmosphere. Many times employees would say, "If we could just get by a day without nagging customers. . . . " The employees were not advocates and cheerleaders for their customers. It was not the way to assuage Jim's minitantrums.

What has Jim done with his newfound marketing wisdom? The manufacturer representatives were told to bring ideas on how Jim could find out more about his customers. If the idea didn't answer that issue, it was rejected. It took a while to get the reps' creative juices working in the right direction, but after the first idea was implemented, more good ideas started flowing. Within 60 days of his search for knowing his customer better, Jim held a "trunk show" for a new line of candles and held a contest for naming different scented candles. I'm not sure I would have attended this promotion, but 75 customers did and Jim has their names and addresses. Jim now knows his best candle customers. Four more product promotions are planned, each with the sole purpose of finding his best customers for these products.

Jim invited 10 candle customers to return for a morning brain-storming session to discuss how to expand the sales of candles and related items. He's got some great ideas and can't wait to begin the process of changing the store to satisfy his customers.

Jim has changed and so have his employees. How do Jim's turned-on, customer-obsessed employees show their loyalty to the customer? Bad news (customer concerns or complaints) is now good news, and is sought and rewarded. They don't want any "nice" customers hurting their business. Each employee calls 10 customers a week to see if they are satisfied with their purchase. It doesn't matter if the purchase was $4 or $400.

Good marketing is as much attitude as tactic. When a positive customer attitude becomes part of the store's everyday operation, it's easy to create the right marketing tactics.

GETTING DOWN TO BUSINESS

Applying Marketing Principles to Your Business

MARKETING PRINCIPLE 1
Marketing starts with customers—the marketer works backward from the customer to the product, customer to services, customer to warranty, and customer to sales presentation.

1. What are your store hours? _____

    What hours would your customers prefer? _____

2. Do your customers like the way your salespeople dress? ____

3. What does your store guarantee for what you sell? Is it well publicized? (This does not include manufacturers'

    warranties.) _____

    _____

    _____

4. Do you have negative policies (bounced-check fee, down-payment policy, return policy, etc.) taped to the wall behind

    the register? Why? _____

    _____

5. Do you know your customers as well as you know your

    suppliers? _____

    List five things you would do to correct that problem.

    a. _____

    b. _____

    c. _____

    d. _____

    e. _____

6. Are your employees more loyal to your customers than to

    you? _____

Without creating anarchy, how would you build a "customer-

loyal" team of employees? _____

_____

_____

7. If you were to start your business today as a new venture, would

it look and behave like your existing store? _____

_____

_____

What five things would you do to move closer to the "new
venture" look?

a. _____

b. _____

c. _____

d. _____

e. _____

MARKETING PRINCIPLE 2

2.

Marketing is part of every employee's job. An organization that reflects this is structured from the outside/inside. The outside (customer) determines what the inside (organization) looks like and how it operates.

The organization of a business that reflects this marketing fact is shown in Figure 6-1.

Fred Smith, chairman of Federal Express, conceived of this upside-down organization ladder as his company grew. In Federal Express, the managers constantly listen to and implement suggestions from the frontline personnel who deal with the customers. Consequently, many of the technological and service innovations have come from customer suggestions to frontline personnel, not through the traditional top-down management-knows-all channels.

Consider Nordstrom. Its organization reflects a marketing commitment. Its frontline sales associates can resolve almost any issue on the spot. Customers are satisfied quickly. The organization

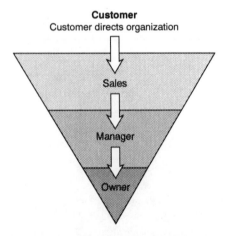

Figure 6-1. A customer-oriented company.

reflects the way the customer wants to be treated, not the way some accountant would want the complaint resolved with management oversight and review.

In a marketing organization, the customer is the most important person, not the owner, and all decisions reflect that commitment.

Unfortunately, most retail organizations look like Figure 6-2.

Sears is a good example of an organization that turned inward and lost touch with its customers. Sears invented "Satisfaction guaranteed or your money back," but it directed its activity inward to the company, to bulletins and policies, until that phrase rang hollow and Sears lost many customers.

Sears established so many policies to catch the 2% that were going to cheat the company anyway, that the 98% who had legitimate complaints could not get the simplest issue resolved quickly. The customer was always taken care of, but the process was so painful and cumbersome, and so many people reviewed the decision, that by the time the problem was corrected, the customer was furious about how long it had taken.

In any organization, there is a natural pull inward, away from the customer. Fight it!

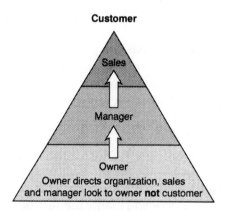

Figure 6-2. Traditional organization.

A Personal View of a Great Marketing Organization

I had an experience that attests to Marketing Principle 2. I was waiting to return a tie my wife bought at Nordstrom. The man in front of me wanted to return a pair of sunglasses that he received as a gift. He had been told they had been purchased at Nordstrom. The clerk (associate) suggested that the glasses had been purchased elsewhere, but the customer insisted they were from Nordstrom.

To avoid offending a known repeat Nordstrom customer, she let him exchange the glasses for a pair he preferred.

I asked her if the sunglasses were from Nordstrom. She said, "No, I recognize the brand; it's sold by our competitor at the other end of the mall. He really thought they were bought from here, and I'm sure he'll be back many times to buy from Nordstrom."

Wow!

My basic instinct was to begin to disrobe and receive full credit for my Sears ensemble, but I resisted.

View from Main Street

Principle 2 is not about the customer deciding who does what in your company. It is about how your employees do what they do and what their relationship is with the customer. No job in a Main Street retail store should be totally isolated from the customer. All should be structured to have some productive contact with the customer. I'll use Bob's Car Wash of Roseville, California, to demonstrate this.

There are seven car washes on a five-mile stretch of Sunrise Boulevard in Roseville. I estimate that Bob's does 50% of all the business. Why? Each car wash appears to have the same type of cleaning equipment and hires teenagers. Bob's is special, though.

A greeter welcomes each customer. The cashier thanks the customer for choosing Bob's and asks if the customer is new to Bob's. If so, the customer receives a professional brochure about Bob's and a discount card for repeat business. The waiting area is immaculate. Children are taken on a tour of the car-wash operation, the teenagers wear a Bob's shirt, and the last employee in contact with the customer says, "Thank you," asks if the coupon has been punched, gives the child a button, and waves good-bye—every day, every time, all the time.

A questionnaire is sent to every customer for every transaction. Bob asks for ideas on how to improve the operations and if customers have promotional suggestions. One of the most successful promotions is the "Bob's working on the line, so let's keep him busy" on Saturday. He'll work, even if it's through lunch, until there is a break in the line. Customers enjoy seeing Bob exhausted but smiling.

If a customer does not return within three months, Bob's mails a reminder and asks the customer to come by for some special promotion.

Bob's uses a computer to track and keep in touch with customers. He uses customers to improve his operation and help create fun promotions (not just price discounts). Bob also has trained his people to be always pleasant to the customer so that the Bob's experience is always enjoyable.

Bob's selling prices are no higher than the competition, but his results are the envy of all the car washes on Sunrise Boulevard.

GETTING DOWN TO BUSINESS

Applying Marketing Principles to Your Business

MARKETING PRINCIPLE 2
Marketing is part of every employee's job. An organization that reflects this is structured from the outside/inside. The outside (customers) determines what the inside (organization) looks like and how it operates.

1. Review your last 10 company operation policies. Do they have anything to do with improving your customer relations and marketing to customers? Would your key customers agree these policies create more benefits for them?

   _____

   _____

   _____

2. Write five new policies that will improve the benefits that your key customers want.

    a. Greeting timing cycle

    b. Icebreaker — Names

    c. 24 hr discounts everyday

    d. 99¢ Kids meal with Bev.

    e. Complaints Solved now - Server.

3. How many employees have nothing to do with the customer? Why? What could you do to use some of their time to face the customer?

    _____

    _____

    _____

4. How long does it take you to resolve a complaint?

    _____

5. What do you have to do to resolve complaints in the time the customer would want? _____

    _____

    _____

    _____

    _____

6. For those who install products: What is more important to your
    key customers, installing the product right away or installing
    the product on the date you promised?

    _____

    _____

    _____

    _____

7. Evaluate your performance against what you believe your key
    customers want in Question 6. How can you improve on this
    promise?

    _____

    _____

    _____

    _____

MARKETING PRINCIPLE 3

3.
Marketing is discipline: creating a few meaningful benefits (better than the competition) directed at specific customer groups. This is the ultimate risk in marketing. Be something special to a specific target (customer), otherwise you will be nothing to everyone.

Smart Main Street retailers understand they can *sell* to anybody who walks in their store, but they cannot *market* to anybody or everybody. Delicatessen marketing (offering a little bit of something for this customer group, a little bit of something else for another customer group) is lethal. Smart Main Street retailers know that all customers are not of equal importance to their success.

The risk in marketing is choosing specific groups of customers and directing your limited marketing budget toward them. The other potential customer groups are treated with benign neglect. Sure, you'll happily sell to them, but you will only market to (find and keep) your selected (targeted) customer groups.

You must create benefits that are uniquely appropriate for the groups you have chosen and disregard other benefits that other groups might want. The key (core) customer is always right, but not all customers are right for your business. Some customers are not right because they will want you to offer different benefits than the ones you have devised for your key (core) customer groups.

Those benefits that you create for your key customers must be bigger, better, and more compelling than any your competition offers. These benefits will become, over time, your image, your identity, and your position in the marketplace.

Your store has a position in the marketplace. Customers and noncustomers perceive your store in a certain way. Here are a few examples of how this works:

a. Wal-Mart is known as a low-price retailer for items that are purchased frequently during the year.

b. Nordstrom is known for exceptional customer service.

c. Toys-"R"-Us is known for the widest assortment of toys under one roof.

d. Blockbuster video is known for the widest selection of movies.

e. Walt Disney is known for clean, family-oriented entertainment. When Disney decided to advance PG-13 and R-rated movies under the Walt Disney name for the 18–24 age set, the movies bombed. Bambi and naughty talk did not please the core Disney customer, and the 18–24-year-olds didn't believe Disney movies were right for them. That is why Disney invented the name Touchstone. You may be sure that the first Touchstone movie, *Splash*, would have failed if it had been produced by Disney. (It was produced by Disney, but no one knew it, and it was a smash hit.)

As a successful retailer, you defend at all costs the superior benefits you are delivering to your key customers. It is not good enough to offer benefits equal to your competition. The Latin base of "competitive" means to win, not tie!

A Personal View of Targeting

I refereed high school soccer in a small rural community in Oregon that was unfamiliar with the game, so it really was more like a combination of football and wrestling using a round ball.

After one particularly ugly game, I decided to stop for a drink at a local tavern. When I opened the door, I knew I had made a mistake. There I stood in black polyester shorts, with white-trimmed knee-high socks, a black shirt, and a whistle around my neck. Thirty loggers and bikers stared in my direction.

With great gusto I asked the bartender for a glass of Chardonnay wine. That was not the drink of choice in this tavern and the group hooted and hollered. I remembered my theory that not all customers are right for a business, and I ran for my life!

View from Main Street

It is every Main Street retailer's worst nightmare: A major competitor is coming to town. In this case, a major mall was coming and John Norris, owner of Norris Shoes (located on Main Street in Medford, Oregon), knew that the mall would contain at least 20 businesses selling shoes. The better-known names were Foot Locker, Florsheim, Track 'N Trail, and JCPenney.

Norris Shoes had been around for 40 years. It sold a little bit of everything to everybody including running shoes, but only one-tenth of what Foot Locker would offer; some hiking boots, but only one-tenth of what Track 'N Trail would offer; and conservative women's shoes, but only. . . . You get the picture. Norris Shoes had successfully marketed for many years with the delicatessen approach but John knew he had to change to face the new competition.

The decision was not easy. Medford was a small town with a population of 36,000 and John and his employees had fitted entire families with shoes. He knew many of his repeat customers by name, and worried that if he stopped offering children's shoes, the entire family would go elsewhere, or if he stopped selling cowboy boots, shoppers would head to the mall and never return.

The first thing John did was leave town to "shop" his new competitors. He practiced open spying. He talked to customers when they left the competitors, and he learned the strengths of each store, the key brands they carried, the key price points, and their display and selling techniques. He was ready to analyze his own business against this new backdrop.

John had never caught the direct-marketing bug, but he did record his sales by product type and did have an extensive customer list, although he did not know what customers had purchased. His choice was clear: either expand the offerings in low-selling product categories (children's shoes, adult exercise and running shoes, women's dress shoes, better dress shoes for men, and cowboy boots) or drop them and increase the assortment, size offering, and inventory dollars in the best-selling categories. He chose the latter and decided to go from delicatessen marketing to narrowcasting. It was the right move.

Prior to the mall, John Norris felt Norris Shoes had an image of a well-run, family shoe store that offered personable service and knowledgeable salespeople. He emphasized "family shoe store," a kind of cradle-to-the-grave marketing program. This image was more in John's mind than the customer's. The new mall forced him to take a close look at his image, from the customer's view. When he did, he found that most of his customers didn't take their children to his store. The 13-year-old Air Jordan customer with baseball hat on backward and testosterone coursing through his veins, and a senior citizen looking for a comfortable shoe and worried about her bunions were not a realistic shopping duo. He could market to either, but not to both. He chose the seniors.

When the mall opened, John had half as many styles as he offered before the mall, but twice the assortment, variety, and size offerings in his key lines. This was narrowcasting at its best. John informed his customers of the changes with smart direct-mail campaigns. Every mailing asked the customers to come in and see the changes and when they did, they were asked to fill out a questionnaire about what additional improvements they would like to see.

John experienced a 6% decrease for the first "mall" year. Four other downtown shoe merchants made no changes and went out of business. "We've been here 60 years and our customers know and like us, and we aren't changing," one proud owner said about the impending mall and what he was going to do. He stood his ground and his business vanished, 60 years and all.

In his second mall year, John fine-tuned the benefits the customers were seeking from him. He knew because 400 had completed the questionnaire. He changed his store hours. He opened two hours earlier than the mall stores and added more sales help at lunchtime (11–2), just as the mall stores were sending their salespeople to lunch. (Mall stores are notorious for having a skeleton crew at this busy time.) He moved a well-run shoe-repair shop into his store and continued to expand services to the key customers, but he did not expand the style offerings.

John Norris took the ultimate risk in marketing. He became the best marketer for his key customers and stopped dabbling with the others. He listened to his customers. *Dominance and narrowcasting go hand in hand.*

GETTING DOWN TO BUSINESS

Applying Marketing Principles to Your Business

MARKETING PRINCIPLE 3
Marketing is discipline: creating a few meaningful benefits (better than the competition) directed at specific customer groups. This is the ultimate risk in marketing. Be something special to a specific target (customer), otherwise you will be nothing to everyone.

1. What is your store's image or identity in your mind?

   _____

   _____

   _____

2. What is your store's image or identity in your key customers' minds?

   _____

   _____

   _____

3. If they are not the same, should they be?

   _____

   _____

   _____

4. Should you try to change your customers' minds or change your company to meet your customers' perception?

_____

_____

5. Consider your best (most aggressive) competition that is going after your key customer group. What three benefits does it offer customers and what three benefits do you offer? Who executes the specific benefits better for the key customer group?

        Your Competition   You

    a. _____

    b. _____

    c. _____

    _____

6. How can you improve, widen, or deepen the three most important benefits so that they will clearly become, without any doubt, your image and no one else will have that position?

    _____

    _____

    _____

    _____

    _____

    _____

MARKETING PRINCIPLE 4

4.

You must know and describe your core customer: the customer who is most apt to buy your product most often. This core customer should move up the loyalty ladder and become an advocate. When you know your core customer, you are taking the key step toward marketing wisdom!

In Marketing Principle 3, I discussed the need to create benefits for and commit all your marketing efforts toward a few customer groups. The *core customer* is the largest and most important customer group. If you complete a simple customer sales analysis, you will discover quickly that very few customers (or customer types) generate a very large percentage of your sales. The 20/80 rule is fundamental to all aspects of marketing: Your core customer will represent no more than 20% of total customers, but generate close to 80% of your sales.

The 20/80 rule (Figure 6-3) is true for every Main Street retailer. There are no exceptions to this marketing and statistical fact.

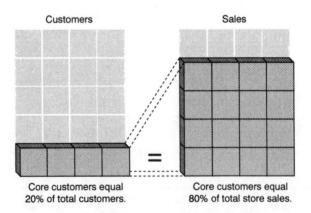

Figure 6-3. The 20/80 rule.

You create your core benefits for your core customer. These benefits are uniquely right for the core customer, but will not be quite right for the other customer groups. That is okay. When you consistently deliver core benefits to core customers, they will find more core customers for your store.

Every business has core customers. When you know who they are, what they buy, and what benefits they seek, you will know how to best serve them. Their loyalty will be expressed in repeat business and by becoming advocates.

Waldenbooks, the bookstore chain, analyzed its sales and found that 20% of its customers were heavy readers and generated 74% of total sales. So it offered the 20% (core customer) a membership in the Preferred Club. In this club, customers automatically received a 10% discount on all purchases and an additional 5% for every $100 spent. Preferred Club is Waldenbooks' successful program for keeping core customers happy and making them "clients."

American Airlines was the first airline to discover its core customer. A small percentage of air travelers, mostly businesspeople, represent more than 70% of all airline ticket sales. Most business travelers fly regularly, so, American decided to offer a frequent-flyer program to entice the business travelers to become clients. This program now is linked with hotels, rental cars, and credit cards. Today, all airline competitors have a frequent-flyer program. The American Airlines program is the classic example of understanding the core customer and matching benefits to them.

Pamper Your Core Customers

Core customers are people who shop at your store regularly because they like how the store is operated and the store fits their needs. They are loyal and see no reason to shop elsewhere. It is unforgivable ever to lose a core customer.

The most successful businesses have programs to pamper their best customers and are always looking for other ways to prove their loyalty to their core customers.

Spiegel catalog brags that 25% of its new customers come from the legion of core customers who are advocates for the catalog company. Those advocates send in names of friends who they think would like to be a Spiegel customer. Spiegel sends the prospective customer a minicatalog, and more than 75% become customers. That is not surprising. Core customers have friends who are like themselves and exhibit the same buying habits.

Spiegel knows that its continued improvement in core benefits for core customers is rewarded with a large number of advocates who deliver to Spiegel names of people who are like themselves—other potential core customers. Any Main Street retailer can create many advocates for their store by creatively staying in touch with core customers. (Section IV, Keeping Customers, is all about creating advocates for your business.)

Don't Confuse Your Core Customer

In 1985, Coca-Cola was trying to find a replacement for Tab. Coke found a sweeter formula and was so happy with it that the company launched Diet Coke. Diet Coke sales far exceeded their expectations. Based on that, the company decided to change the taste of its main product, Coke.

The new Coke was met with incredible resistance from its core customers—the baby boomers. At that time, the baby boomers were 29 to 44 years old. They had grown up with Coke. Within three months of the introduction of the new Coke, the baby boomers forced the company to bring back the original Coca-Cola, which is now called Coca-Cola Classic. And guess what? Coca-Cola Classic generates 20.1% market share and the newer, sweeter Coke holds a pitiful 1.4% share.

The Coca-Cola executives were very confused by these results. They had administered more than 200,000 taste tests to ensure their new Coke was the taste that consumers wanted. But the image in the minds of the core customer was of a product that had not been altered in 90 years, whose very name meant consistent quality and taste. To Coca-Cola's surprise, that image was far more powerful than the benefit of a slightly sweeter taste. When customers who had liked the new taste in the taste test were later asked why they didn't buy the new Coke, the common reply was, "I like Coke just the way it is." Perception is more powerful than reality!

Don't confuse your core customer, but if you do, apologize and get back in their good graces.

Don't Be Distracted from the Core Benefits

There are always temptations to change products or policies to satisfy a customer or management request. Do so only after you have asked your core customers and received their approval. Foolish? Ask Kmart.

Kmart is a good example of a store that became distracted from the core benefits in an attempt to make more gross profit. Kmart started a program of in-house brands (Jaclyn Smith) to sell at higher prices than the generic items. It started out successfully and they raised the prices. In their search for a higher profit, they forgot about the low-price benefit their core customers expected. When given a chance, the core customers went to Wal-Mart. Many did not return.

If Potential New Core Customers Find You, Love Them Only if They Seek Very Similar Benefits

Bran Flakes accomplished the nearly impossible. For years, older Americans were the core customers for this product. They ate the cereal for health reasons, not taste. Bran Flakes helped keep older Americans regular.

As the baby boomers grew up, they saw the benefit in Bran Flakes as healthy living: low in cholesterol, high fiber, and lots of vitamins. (This is known as the Smuckers school of marketing. "If it tastes like sand and chews like grit, it's gotta be good for you.") Baby boomers started buying Bran Flakes and sales skyrocketed. Bran Flakes did not want to disregard this potential new core customer, 70 million strong and *six* times the size of the old core customer group.

Bran Flakes realized that its brand name stood for *good health* for both these customer groups. The image of the brand and the benefits sought were the same—healthy living. Bran Flakes simply expanded its definition of healthy living to include the baby boomers' definition. The product didn't change. These baby boomers now have become the core customers by virtue of their size. And in 10 years, Bran Flakes will become the breakfast brand for older Americans—older baby boomers, that is. Regularity will be reinvented!

Don't Betray Your Core Customer

It is almost impossible to go away from your core customer and build a new customer base with different benefits and still be successful.

When People Express started in the airline business, it went from zero to $1 billion in 18 months. It was a fabulous success. The core customer was the vacationer, not the business traveler. Luggage generally arrived days after the flight, or so it seemed, but People Express had the right benefits for its core customer: extremely low prices for vacationing families, leaving at somewhat inconvenient times from convenient airports. These were bare-bones, no-frills flights. Salted peanuts were dinner and you didn't get a second helping.

People Express then decided to seek more business travelers. These customers wanted different benefits: reliable luggage delivery, computerized ticketing, meals, a frequent-flyer program, convenient departure times, and first class. The airline raised prices, attempted to deliver those new benefits, lost its core customer, and did not attract the business traveler. People Express quickly went bankrupt.

The success of Bran Flakes does not suggest that People Express wasn't as smart. The situations were different. Business travelers had avoided People Express because they sought completely different benefits than People Express had ever offered, and no amount of persuading could change their image of People Express. For Bran Flakes, a new customer group "found" them, and the benefit they sought was the same as the benefit the product was delivering to the original core customer. All Bran Flakes had to do was change some of their marketing tactics to explode the sales with this new core customer.

The difference between Bran Flakes' success and People Express's failure is marketing. Bran Flakes listened "naively" to customers and found a new group who were starting to buy their product. It worked backward from the customer. People Express decided to change its entire operation for a new customer who had shown no interest in its service. That's not marketing, it's wishful thinking.

View from Main Street

Jacksonville, Oregon (home of Mimi's Yarn shop and Liquor store, whose admonition over the cash register says, "Don't drink and darn") is a very small, old mining town (population 1,800). Most of the retail trade depends on tourism.

Gary West Meats sells a unique, moist beef jerky, smoked turkeys, hams, and complementary sauces and condiments. They are a well-established family business. Tourists typically visited between June and October, made one purchase, and returned home. Gary West Meats hoped the customers would return the next year, but that was the extent of its marketing. Some tourists said they would like to buy the beef jerky for friends as Christmas presents. The store gave customers its phone number, but few called.

Dee West, the marketing whiz for the store, decided to find out who was the store's best customer. For one year, every customer was asked for their address, if they were repeat visitors to the area, and how they had learned about Gary West Meats. Dee found two core customer groups of equal size but totally different shopping habits: (1) the local customer who visited the store four times a year and made an average purchase of $19; (2) the repeat tourist from northern California who visited once, average purchase of $47.50. These two core customer groups represented 62% of total sales. (This system of collecting marketing information was simple and straightforward and the customers did not feel inconvenienced.)

Dee decided to concentrate on northern California tourists. She wrestled with the problem: How can we increase the sales to tourists, even though they only visit once? The answer was clear:

Don't try to sell them 10 pounds of jerky, instead of two, when they make their one visit, but rather create a modest catalog from which the tourist could buy gifts in December for their friends who had not visited Jacksonville. And if the tourists/customers wanted to buy something for themselves at the same time, that was just fine.

This program became a great success, and the number of customers in Dee's data file increased exponentially—one tourist buys once in the summer and in the winter buys two gifts for neighborhood friends. Three names for one visit! Next year all three would get the catalog. It was like the Amway of beef jerky!

Like any good retailer, Dee West "kinda" knew the importance of the tourist, but when she acquired the real numbers and names, she was ready to build a new, prosperous catalog business for one of her core customers, the tourist.

The Core Is the Heart and Essence of the Store

Every business, regardless of size or competence, has a core customer. Sears does (it just can't find them), IBM does, the chiropractor does, and so do you. When you determine who the core customer is and what that customer really wants from your store, and you deliver those benefits, you will enhance the image and essence of your business.

The principle of knowing your core customers, and offering benefits they want, goes to the heart of retail marketing. My experience has been that most Main Street retailers "kinda" know who their core customer is. The "Oh, yeah, they represent a lot of business" marketing knowledge is not good enough.

If you know who your core customers are and listen to them regularly, you will never lose touch with the benefits they are seeking. This alone will make you a unique retailer in your town.

For a start-up retail store, you must decide who you think will be your core customer, before, *I repeat, before,* you choose a location. To do otherwise is to create a tremendous hardship on your business from the start. Far too often the new entrepreneur decides on a location that has great foot traffic, is in a new strip mall, or is convenient to the owner and friends. Those are not good enough reasons to choose a location. If the major tenant in the strip mall (it doesn't matter if the major tenant is a grocery store or tanning salon) has a core customer who is different than yours, you have made a disastrous marketing decision.

Existing retailers must commit to learning who their core customers are and what benefits they seek. I'll show you how to do this in Section III, Finding Customers.

GETTING DOWN TO BUSINESS

Applying Marketing Principles to Your Business

MARKETING PRINCIPLE 4
You must know and describe your core customer: the customer who is most apt to buy your product most often. This core customer should move up the loyalty ladder and become an advocate. When you know your core customer, you are taking the key step toward marketing wisdom!

1. Do you know your core customer for key sectors of your business? _____

2. Describe each core customer.

   a. _____

   b. _____

   c. _____

   d. _____

   _____

3. What percentage of business does your core customer generate?

   a. _____

b. _____

c. _____

d. _____

4. Do you know where your core customers live? Describe.

a. _____

b. _____

c. _____

d. _____

MARKETING PRINCIPLE 5

5.
Core concept expanded: People with similar tastes, values, and demographics buy similar things . . . usually.

Your core customers are so powerful that they act as a major force in your business and affect the entire marketing of it. The 20/80 rule, which applies to customers and the products they buy, works for the following product factors:

1. Core products—
2. Core price points⌐
3. Core unit producers⌐

Core Products

An analysis of any retail store or service always finds that the 20/80 rule applies to products as well as customers. Very few items or skus (stock keeping units) deliver an inordinately large percentage of your volume. In 1973, Sears Roebuck recognized this fact. Only 5.3% of the 16,000 skus in a typical Sears store generated 43.2% of the store's total volume. Sears called these high-volume items "basic-basic" items. Today, Sears has fewer total skus, but the basic-basic items now generate more than 50% of a store's volume.

The Main Street retailer is the same, but it cannot be passive with these core items. Never give equal treatment to products in display, inventory, promotion, and sales training. Bias your marketing efforts for the core products.

Any customer who walks into a retail store should quickly be able to recognize what the core products are for the store. The dominance of the displays, the depth of the inventory, and sales presentation should readily identify the core products for the customer.

Retailers often take the core products for granted and continually look for newer and different products. That attitude leads to poor displays and constant out-of-stocks of core items. It is unforgivable to be out of stock of a core product—ever. Many retailers tell me, "I just can't keep these in stock. They're my best-sellers. I ordered 24, and I was already out of stock, so I doubled the order again and ordered 48, and look, I am still out of stock. I just don't understand." That retailer should have ordered 480 of those items and canceled orders on marginal selling products.

Always be out of stock of noncore items first but never, never be out of stock of core items. Core items are bought by core customers. Don't disappoint them.

Expanding the Core

It is always best to expand the core products before expanding into other product types.

Lands' End, the direct-marketing company in Wisconsin, started selling button-down shirts in a 12-page catalog. It was very successful, so Lands' End decided to expand its product offering. Rather than add ties, belts, and slacks, it wisely expanded around the core:

Core products	Long-sleeve, button-down shirts: 6 solid colors—12 sizes
Expanded offerings	Long-sleeve, button-down shirts: 12 solid colors—24 sizes 6 stripes—12 sizes 4 plaids—12 sizes 2 new fiber blends—solid color monogram Athletic cut Short sleeve: 6 solid colors—4 sizes 4 stripes—4 sizes

Lands' End doubled the number of pages and yet still *only* offered button-down shirts. Only after establishing its core with such dominance did it move into other menswear. Lands' End first expanded all the opportunities of its core product and by doing this made clients out of existing core customers, and found a tremendous number of new customers, all like the core group.

Core Price Points

A review of your sales by average price point will show that, like products and customers, a few price points will represent a very large percentage of your sales. These are your core price points. A typical floor-covering store might sell most installed carpet at $19.99 and $24.99 per yard. The core customers believe $19.99 and $24.99 are where they receive the best value. This floor-covering store should have the most samples, displays, and inventory committed to these two price points.

If the core price points are the most expensive in that product line, the retailer should add more expensive items. Take the floor-covering store as an example. If $19.99 and $24.99 are the *best selling* and *highest price,* the store should add products at $27.99 and higher. The reason: Allow customers to comparison shop in your store for a full range of prices, so they won't feel the need to go elsewhere.

You should have an equal number of products above and below your core price points, but the largest number of products, items, and skus should be committed to the core price points.—

Your offerings and sales by product type should resemble a bell curve (Figure 6-4).

Obviously, you can't achieve a perfect bell curve for all your product offerings, but you must evaluate your offerings by price point on a regular basis. All retailers are pressured by suppliers to buy new and different items at myriad price points. In a short period of time (even with good intentions), you are offering products at price points that don't reflect your core customer's buying habits. Having the right number of products at the core price points is another way of pampering the core customer.

Core Unit Producers

Most retail sales analysis and product ranking are done by dollar sales. If you sell $.99 items and products for $100, you also must

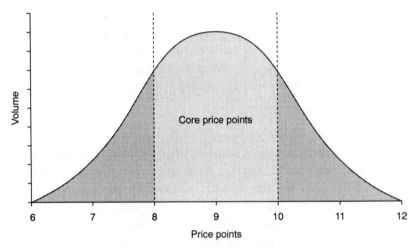

Figure 6-4. Product offerings by price point.

know your core unit producers. The inexpensive product might not show up as a significant dollar-selling item, but many customers are buying the product. It must be treated the same as the core items based on dollar sales.

In a Sears hardware department, the best-selling dollar items are the more expensive electric hand tools. However, if the customer comes in for a screwdriver, nails, and a bracket and the store has none of them, what are the chances the customer will come back to buy the drill or sander? I can tell you, as a former customer service manager for Sears, there is one rule in customer disappointment when it comes to out-of-stocks: The smaller and less expensive the item, the worse the customer's ire. The Sears core customers were unhappy and unforgiving for the store's not having the small items they wanted to buy. They resented the inconvenience. It is the same for your store.

A Personal View of the Core Concept

I graduated from a well-known engineering college as an English major. Few companies were impressed with my schooling, but, God bless them, Sears thought I was quite a find. I joined Sears

Roebuck and Co. as a manager trainee. After six months of watching people do things and thinking, "I can do better than that," I became the paint department manager.

The first thing I did was organize the interior paint section. In those days, all paint was premixed, so I displayed our interior paint in 26 rows, with each row containing a different color. It was so well-designed, it was almost poetic.

When the store manager reviewed my department, he asked why I had one row for each color. I answered, "Symmetry." He said, "Symmetry never sold anything. Is that all they taught you in college? Go get the sales figures and tell me what percentage of interior paint sold is white and off-white." I returned and told him that 64% of our sales were white and off-white, and he told me, in no uncertain terms, "Our core customer buys white and antique white, not symmetry. Change the display so it reflects that balance of sale and get it done today." I did.

Our department experienced a 200% increase for the next three months and I was promoted. I have never, ever believed in symmetry since then.

The core customer buys core products and that should determine the display and inventory. Symmetry be damned.

View from Main Street

Every retailer has core products. It does not matter whether you're big or small, smart, or a hit-and-miss retailer, you attract a certain kind of person who buys the same things most of the time. The core concept is inextricably entwined—customer and product. Core products and customers are the essence and heart of your Main Street retail store.

From a product standpoint, if you want to find more core customers or sell more product to existing core customers (the ones that have bought from you), expanding the number of brands, sizes, styles, or ancillary products of core products is the best first step.

Placesetters, a Williams-Sonoma look-alike in Medford, Oregon, approached the new mall issue in an entirely different way than Norris Shoes. Meier & Frank (a Northwest department store chain) was one of the anchors and had kitchenware, dinnerware, and linens and furnishings sections, about *three times* the size of Placesetters. Prior to arriving in Medford, Meier & Frank completed an aggressive credit program: If you could spell any part of their name, including "&," you received a Meier & Frank credit card. There was no department store in town and Sears was the best general merchandiser. After so many years of product and marketing deprivation, you can imagine the excitement created by the Meier & Frank credit-card blitz and its impending arrival.

Placesetters opened its doors six years prior to the mall and was very successful. It owned the better kitchen and dinner business in southern Oregon. Placesetters was a beautifully displayed store and, with its new products and ideas, was a fun place to shop. It deserved to be a successful $1 million retailer; its success was not luck.

Unfortunately, Placesetters believed its own press. The owners thought they were without peers. (A good retailer should always have a large dose of self-doubt and be forever critical of their operation. That's the best way to keep up with, understand, and accept your customers' change in buying habits.) Placesetters had built a business that was the envy of the town and customer loyalty was never in doubt, or so it thought. In their misbegotten self-importance, Placesetters' owners decided that Meier & Frank was so big, bureaucratic, and inflexible that Meier & Frank's advertising would drive customers to Placesetters once they saw how ordinary Meier & Frank's offerings were. Placesetters decided not to change anything, that it would buy more inventory, and plan for an 18% increase the first 90 days after the mall opened. That is how Placesetters prepared for the new competition. There was no competitive analysis, no core customer and product analysis of their own store, no discussion with their own customers—just good, old-fashioned gut work, cockiness, and pride.

As Shakespeare said, "Pride goeth before the fall." And fall it did. Placesetters had a 35% decrease in sales against an 18% increase in inventory and couldn't pay for the excess inventory or for advertising to try to sell all the overbuys. It was very sad, but predictable. When asked what products didn't sell, one of the partners said, "They all are down equally." In other words, cappuccino makers were off 35%, the same as fine bone china. Although I did not calculate the numbers, I know that's not true. In most cases they ran out of their core items, but sold little else.

Placesetters' failure was preordained. It did not stay close to and communicate with its core customer. When it should have reduced the many small lines of slow-selling products, and concentrated on core products (narrowcasting), since that is what the core customers buy, it bought new products, never carried before, and opened an eating area in the center of the store.

Placesetters presumed core-customer loyalty, but frustrated them with all the changes away from the products they had been buying. Meier & Frank catered to its targeted core customers who were the same as Placesetters'. In three times the store space, Meier & Frank offered *fewer* products, but far more colors, sizes, and brands. Its core product presentations were impressive. Placesetters was de-emphasizing core products to give space to a lunch area. It was no contest. Placesetters never came back and has since vanished from the scene.

Rules for Core Products

Inventory management is beyond the scope of this book, but here are some important rules to follow to be sure you best market your core products for your core customers:

1. Establish lists of unit core and dollar-volume core products. The core products should represent at least 50% of unit or dollar sales. Order all (unit and dollar-volume) core products on two-week intervals. Establish a minimum low stock (ordering point) for each core product. *Never, never, never* be out of stock of core products.
2. Dominantly display core products in more than one section of the store.
3. In all sales training meetings, cover basic training about core products.
4. If a new product begins to sell at the rate of existing core products, order four times what you have been ordering and treat it as a core product.

5. Never reduce inventory or drop core products, unless their sales decline 20%.

6. Review gross profit of core products on a quarterly basis. Don't let profit margins slip on these best-sellers.

7. Advertise core products regularly. For major events, use core unit producers to create store traffic.

GETTING DOWN TO BUSINESS

Applying Marketing Principles to Your Business

MARKETING PRINCIPLE 5
Core concept expanded: People with similar tastes, values, and demographics buy similar things . . . usually.

1. Do you know the five best-selling products in the largest broad market you serve? List them.

   a. ___CF_____

   b. ___Grand Slam_____

   c. _____

   d. _____

   e. _____

2. Do you have more than one display of these five key products?

   Y   N   If not, why?

   a. _____

   b. _____

c. _____

d. _____

e. _____

3. Do you know your core price point?

   a. _____

   b. _____

   c. _____

   4. What percentage of sales do your core price points deliver?

   a. _____

   b. _____

   c. _____

5. How can you maximize the cores for profit?

_____

_____

_____

_____

_____

_____

MARKETING PRINCIPLE 6

6.
The marketer defines the business in customer terms, not industry jargon. Always ask, "Yes, I know that's the way it's been done, but how would the customer want it?"

Define your business in terms of your key customer groups, not how the industry would describe it.

It is often said that if the railroads understood they were in the transportation business rather than the railroad business, they would be stronger today. The movie industry lost tremendous ground to TV because Hollywood officials thought they were in the movie business, rather than the entertainment business.

In the laundromat business, the owner's main concern is dependable, long-lasting cleaning equipment. Customers expect the washers and dryers to work, but they perceive going to the laundromat as incredibly boring. Newer, bigger, brighter machines mean nothing surrounded by three old magazines, two plastic chairs, and a black-and-white TV.

Not surprisingly, a college student recognized the customer's perception of this experience and started the well-known franchise Duds and Suds: a combination laundromat and bar. Some people spent more time in the suds section and forgot theirs duds, but the idea of defining the business in customer terms was excellent.

Most floor-covering specialty stores sell and install floor covering. If these stores defined their business the way the customer would like, it would be: "We sell, install, and *service* floor covering." If that were the definition, the retailer would service the sale by also being the professional carpet cleaner in that town. That would satisfy the customer's definition of full service, and nothing else would matter.

In the early 1980s, the auto industry warranties were: Ford, three years or 30,000 miles; GM, four years or 40,000 miles; Chrysler, five years or 50,000 miles; Ford, six years or 60,000 miles; GM, seven years or 70,000 miles. However, the part that was fully warrantied could not be found or fixed and the car would run without it being repaired. This was gutless, created no risk to the automakers, and created no value to the consumer. Japanese automakers realized that customers disliked this silly "war of years," and offered a three-year or 36,000-mile, bumper-to-bumper warranty (almost everything but the windshield washers were included), with the opportunity to extend the warranty another three years for $500. They changed the industry by building value the way the customer wanted it.

The next two examples are of companies that asked their customers what business the customers thought the companies were in and then redirected the entire company to their customers' perception.

Nike thought it was in the running-shoe business and realized only later that customers placed it in the exercise business. Since Nike's entire focus was on running shoes, it missed the growth of jazzercise, aerobic exercise, and biking. But after customer input, Nike dramatically changed course and became very successful.

Better Homes and Gardens started in the magazine business. Market research indicated that its customers thought *Better Homes and Gardens* was not just a magazine, but a company that "disseminated useful information to middle America," and it expanded accordingly. Now *Better Homes and Gardens* sells globes, gardening books, cookbooks, 20 do-it-yourself books, home improvement books, and so on.

To become a truly great company, you must know who you are. Leave nothing to chance. A marketing company questions even the most basic tenet. Basic tenets are always proceeded with a fatherly, "Son, we've always done it that way." A marketing company will say, "Yes, I know that's the way it's been done, but how would the customer want it?"

A great marketing retailer always turns to the customer for answers.

View from Main Street

As a retailer, you probably rely on suppliers and their sales reps for marketing guidance. Don't. They don't know your customers; all they know is their program to get you to sell more of their products. Unless they are willing to help you determine who your core customer is and evaluate your core products, ignore them. Their only value is a free lunch and gossip, neither very good.

The reason I say this about reps is that most retailers take their advice as gospel, but those who solicit and take their customers' advice and direction distinguish themselves as different and better than those who follow the manufacturer. (Different is not always better. I was in a new video store and was confused about the videos' organization. I asked the owner, "How are these videos organized?" He proudly answered, "They're not. We think our customers will like to wander the aisles and be surprised when they find what they are looking for." Huh? Obviously the store never asked potential customers about this display system. Few customers liked the hide-and-seek approach and the store quietly folded after six months.)

It seems that every town has a handful of retailers that are substantially different (in the customer's mind) than others in the same town that sell the same products, even substantially different than the majority of retailers that sell the same product in the state. I don't mean different and dumb like the video store, but different and very successful. I think their success comes from listening and responding to their customers, not the industry. These retail stores aren't glitzier or equipped with the newest technology. They are better in the simplest and most compelling way—from the customer's view.

The totally customer-oriented store builds advocates that no amount of advertising or technology can buy.

Is your store different and smarter? I know you think so, but is it different, smarter, and better from the customer's standpoint? The following stores are:

Knollwood Hamburgers, Yorba Linda, California
"World's Best Hamburgers." Very large hamburgers. French fries with skin on them served in a paper bag. Dirt road, dirt parking, very fast service. Cheaper than McDonalds'. Everything is "world's best" including the salt, mustard, and T-shirts. They were selling shirts long before anybody put their store name on shirts and then sold them. This place looks and acts nothing like the homogenized, fast-food restaurants we love to hate.

The Popcorn Store, Wheaton, Illinois
This 30-year-old store sells the best-tasting popcorn cooked with good old oil. The address is 176½ Front Street (because it is so small: 4 feet wide, 20 feet long). This store's success has nothing to do with new technology, new concept, or anything new; this store's success can only be explained with, "That's how the Wheaton customer would want it."

Haslam's Book Store, St. Petersburg, Florida
Haslam's is a very large, disjointed bookstore. Each new addition to the center building looks like an addition, poorly done. The senior population loves to read and that's to whom Haslam's caters. The store had an incredible selection of seniors' core subjects (spirituality, mysteries, history), and a modest selection of computer and self-improvement books; probably the world's largest supply of used books; personable service; and patient employees—just the way the customer wants it in St. Petersburg.

None of these stores is particularly pretty. In fact they are all un-pretty, but they have distinguished themselves by following their customers' lead.

Everyone claims to listen to their customers, but few really make it work for their business. Big companies understand this principle the least. Think of the favorite, funky, smart retailer in your town. Now consider how GM would love to be funky and smart. You'll see how big is no contest with the smart, customer-oriented business.

If you're a big business and you do something out of the ordinary (like listen to your customers), that's called a paradigm shift. Big words for big businesses, but it's all about the same thing. Consider this two-page General Motors advertisement that ran in a 1994 issue of *Life* magazine:

"Finding out what the customer wants is easy. Doing something about it, that's the hard part."

"Liz Wetzel, a member of the Cadillac Design Team at General Motors, spends a fair amount of time listening to customers react to their ideas. This is not always fun. Human nature being what it is, most people instinctively want to discount views that don't square with their own. Sometimes responding to customer input means scrapping a beloved notion. It can mean costly retooling or a delay in production. So be it. These days at General Motors, the customer isn't just somebody with an opinion. The customer is a colleague with a whole lot of clout."

This, of course, is intellectual prattle and bad advertising combined. Finding out what the customer wants is not easy. In fact, it is always difficult. However, when you do find out what the customer wants, then designing a car or your store is easy. (If it really were so easy to find out what the customer wants, how is it that General Motors took so long to understand the customers' wish for a smaller, fuel-efficient, quality-built car that would last for seven or eight years? Weren't they listening? The Japanese were.) The ultimate irony of all this advertising blather is that today the customer has an opinion and a "whole lot of clout." How has that changed from yesterday? The customer had an opinion, just no clout. GM didn't listen.

All the best specialty store chains started as single stores that were different and better than their competition in their town, sufficiently different in ways the customer appreciated, and the stores knew it because they listened to their customers, not their industry. That's the genius of Crate and Barrel, The Limited, Victoria's Secret, Toys-"R"-Us, Gap, Banana Republic, Tower Records, and many others. And that's the genius of those fabulously successful and sometimes funky Main Street retailers in your town. You should be one of them.

GETTING DOWN TO BUSINESS

Applying Marketing Principles to Your Business

MARKETING PRINCIPLE 6
The marketer defines their business in customer terms, not industry jargon. Always ask, "Yes, I know that's the way it's been done, but how would the customer want it?"

1. Is there a business your customers want you to be in that you are not because the industry doesn't work that way? Name the business.

    _____

    _____

2. List the five reasons you are not in this business.

    a. _____

    b. _____

    c. _____

    d. _____

    e. _____

3. Are any of the above reasons customer reasons, or just business and convenience reasons for your retail store?

    _____

    _____

    _____

4. List the reasons the customers would want you to be in the business and how you could profit from the investment?

    a. _____

    b. _____

c. _____

d. _____

e. _____

5. Apply the question, "Yes, I know that's the way it's been done, but how would the customer want it?" to:

Display _____

_____

Package _____

_____

Pricing _____

_____

Warranty _____

_____

MARKETING PRINCIPLE 7

7.
A marketer speaks in the idiom of the customer, not the industry. A marketer understands that features belong to products and benefits belong to customers.

Principles 6 and 7 go hand in hand. You define your business the way the customer would, and you communicate with your customers in their language. Lawyers, doctors, bankers, and insurance agents are notoriously bad about this. They would rather impress you with their knowledge than share it in a meaningful way. Don't act like them.

Charles Revson of Revlon said, "In the factory we make cosmetics. In the marketplace, we sell hope." Mr. Revson knew what the customers were really buying.

D. Kornfeld, past president of Radio Shack, came up with the same idea, and named his book on advertising, *To Catch a Mouse, Make a Sound Like Cheese.*

Catalog marketing is best at taking product features and creating customer benefits for a well-described, targeted customer group. Look at Lands' End, Sharper Image, Patagonia, Herrington, Spiegel, or Harry and David. Their advertising copy reads like their core customers talk.

See how Lands' End combines product features and clear customer benefits for a cotton dress:

"First, the fabric's unusual. We use a springy 100% combed cotton interlock so soft it borders on luxurious!! This is rare, since probably 95% of T-shirt dresses on the market are made of jersey knit. Now that's fine for a T-shirt you'd throw on with shorts, but we think a dress deserves more substance.

Why combed cotton? Several reasons. Combing the cotton fibers before they're spun into yarn creates a more cushiony loft that other interlock lacks. Also, the yarns drink in these beautiful colors better, hold them longer, so your dress won't look faded after a season's worth of washing. Combed cotton helps control shrinkage, too. Even though our knits have to meet some of the most rigorous standards in the business, all cotton will shrink some. So we size our T-shirt dresses to allow for that."

A specific product feature will create different customer benefits for different customer groups. The same product feature, or the same product, is described differently with different benefits to different customer groups. This is not dishonesty, but an understanding that the benefits one customer derives from the product can be and are different from another customer group.

Knowing core customers and the benefits they seek is the marketing key. You learn the benefits the core customers want by constantly listening to them.

A Personal View of How Not to Create Benefits

For two years (1991–1993) Shaw Industries, the world's largest carpet manufacturer, researched and analyzed the reason for the carpet industry's lack of growth. Its findings were conclusive: People hated to shop for carpet. They loved the product but disliked dealing with retail salespeople. Carpet stores engendered the same trust and confidence as used-car dealers. Customers wanted to buy a more beautiful interior for their home, but got so frustrated and confused with warranty and product claims that many gave up.

Figure 6-5 shows that 30% of potential customers who had decided they were going to buy carpet gave up and did not purchase any carpet. Amazing. They set money aside for carpet. They visited four to seven stores and became so confused and disillusioned that they gave up on carpet, bought a dozen vacuum cleaner bags, and went to Hawaii on vacation—or something like that.

Shaw Industries decided to correct the problem. Along with many other retailers, I was invited to Shaw headquarters in Dalton, Georgia, to see the unveiling of a new brand of carpet: Trustmark.

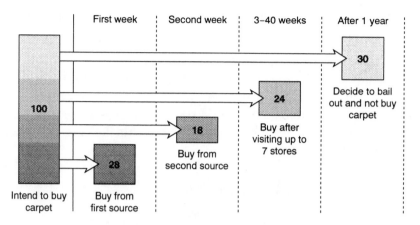

Figure 6-5. How the carpet industry loses customers.

Trustmark? Think of five products that you would associate with Trustmark. I doubt carpet is one of them. Here's my list of products that could use the name:

Guided missiles
Hammer
Condom
Bow and arrow
Golf ball

Yes! Shaw Industries was going to market, advertise, and sell trust. The carpet would follow. To that end, each store that decided to carry Trustmark carpet would have a display system that explained the features of carpet. Shaw called this "full disclosure." It defined the feature and gave the numeric designate for each product.

Example
Product A   *Product B*
Yarn twist—3.5   Yarn twist—3.62

Yarn density—2,740   Yarn density—2,980
Carpet weight—43 oz.   Carpet weight—47 oz.

What a marketing error! The core customer for Trustmark quality carpet is: working women, married, with two children at home and a household income of $40,000+. The reason for purchase is to redecorate one or more rooms. The benefits the core customer is seeking are:

Right color—Subjective concern
Right texture—Subjective concern
Right feel—Subjective concern
Stain resistance—Objective concern
Durability—Objective concern

A fashion product, sold primarily to women, was reduced to meaningless numbers. The aesthetic considerations and benefits customers were seeking from this product were not part of Shaw marketing.

Trustmark was a man's idea of how a man would want a woman to buy carpet. Trust me, it was not a woman's idea of how a woman buys carpet!

Just thank your lucky stars that Shaw has not purchased Victoria's Secret!

View from Main Street

In most bookstores, one of the largest sections is books about computers. Technotalk. The books and their titles are as intimidating as the product. Then along comes *DOS for Dummies*. It is far and away the best-selling computer book for beginners and has spawned many more "Dummy" books for people with computers.

DOS for Dummies speaks in the idiom of the beginner computer user, and the benefit you will receive from using the book is that slowly you will become marginally dumb, maybe even mediocre with your new computer, but that's a lot better than your competence when you went searching for help. The book has graphics and attempts to engage the reader with fun asides, comic book characters, and a you-can-do-it attitude. It is a classic example of talking about the product the way the customer, not the industry, perceives it. That's what Principle 7 is all about.

Every retailer is faced with the same issue—how to describe the benefits of the store and the products in terms the customer understands. Clearly, you must know your core customers before you try to build the benefits. Similar products are perceived differently. When you build your product story from your core customers' vantage point, you almost guarantee the sale.

Bay Irrigation in Rocklin, California, has two core customers: the landscape contractor and the home tuner. The home tuner knows that he can get equipment for less at Kmart or Home Depot, but he wants to be told how to do the job, and he's willing to pay more for the product to get professional help. Bay Irrigation has two customer service lines, with large signs overhead that say "Contractor" and "Retail." For the retail line, there are boards with all the different components for a complete drip system, all attached and identified, forming a miniature drip system. It's idiot-proof. I told them they should call it "Drip for Dummies," but they passed. Funny they're not, but they *are* smart marketers.

This is not only the paint-by-numbers approach—the entire explanation from the salespeople is helpful, nonjudgmental, patient, professional, and understandable. It's okay to say, "thingamajig" and they'll probably know what you're describing. And it doesn't stop there. Bay Irrigation is open nights, Saturdays, and Sundays for the home tuner, and it has a newsletter that provides tips for the simpleminded (my word, not theirs).

Bay Irrigation is open very early in the morning for the contractor and it offers classes for the contractor on new irrigation products and systems. A special credit program is available on large irrigation projects.

Two different core customers seek two different sets of benefits. You can't split the difference, or you'll offend both. Bay Irrigation has done it right.

How do you speak in the idiom of your customers? First, you must listen to your core customers. The rest is imitation.

GETTING DOWN TO BUSINESS

Applying Marketing Principles to Your Business

MARKETING PRINCIPLE 7
A marketer speaks in the idiom of the customer, not the industry. A marketer understands that features belong to products and benefits belong to customers.

1. Take a product that your store sells. Consider your core customer. List the product features and then the benefits that this customer group would derive from that product.

    Product _____

    Core customer description _____

    _____

    _____

    Features _____ Benefits _____

    _____

    _____

    _____

    _____

2. Consider a second customer group for the same product and list what benefits the group would derive from the product.

    Product _____

    Core customer description _____

_____

_____

Features _____ Benefits _____

_____

_____

_____

_____

MARKETING PRINCIPLE 8

8.
The customer's perception of reality *is* reality. To know what the customer's perception is, the marketer must "listen naively."

As a Main Street retailer, you must align your reality with the customer's. Don't try to change the customer's perception; instead, change the way you do business to match the customer's perception.

The president of Delta Airlines said, "The reason we spend so much time on the cleanliness of the interior of the plane is simple: If the customer sees coffee stains on the tray, he believes the engines are not well-maintained." The way the interior of the plane looks has a lot to do with customers' sense of safety and whether they will reach their destination.

David Ogilvy, the modern guru of advertising, tells a story of the power of the customer's perception. He says, "Give the customer a drink of Jim Beam bourbon (an inexpensive brand). Tell them it is Jim Beam. Then give them another drink of Jim Beam bourbon, but this time tell them it is Jack Daniels (a well-known premium brand). Then ask them which one they like." According to Ogilvy, more than 90% will say they like the Jack Daniels better and will wax eloquently about the charcoal filtering, pure Kentucky water, mellowness, and more. The customer tastes images and images create reality, not the other way around, Ogilvy says.

Pepsi-Cola has had the same experience. Back in the 1970s and early 1980s, it launched a very aggressive campaign using taste tests in supermarkets. Customers were asked to drink two different colas without knowing the brand and then they were asked which one they preferred. Of the customers who preferred and usually drank Coke, 75% chose Pepsi in the taste test.

Pepsi-Cola management took this as great news, but sales didn't increase. So they returned to the marketplace and asked Coke customers who preferred Pepsi in the taste test why they had not changed to Pepsi. The most recurring response was, "Oh, I never buy Pepsi, I drink Coke."

People taste images. Images become reality, and most people don't want to change their habits, which will change the reality they know.

As Pepsi knows, listening naively is not easy. Stu Leonard, a well-known supermarket marketer in Connecticut, tells a story of a customer complaint. The customer said, "You don't have fresh fish." The owner's son brought the woman down to the supermarket floor and said, "There is forty feet devoted to fresh fish. It's brought from the harbor every day, it's never frozen, and it's fresh every day. That's fresh fish!" The customer replied, "No, that's not fresh fish." Angrily, the young man said, "Well then show me what fresh fish is." The lady then took the fish out of the cellophane and placed it on the ice and said, "Young man, that's fresh fish."

Listen Naively

How do you listen naively? Hotels use comment cards. Big companies use market research. Smart Main Street retailers use a thank-you card, with a questionnaire, a monthly customer help session to keep the company in line with the customers' perception, and an annual quality-assurance questionnaire sent to all customers.

I will cover how to thank and listen to your core customer in Section IV, Keeping Customers. When you commit to listening to your customer on a regular basis, you will be amazed to find out what the customer is not impressed with. Conversely, the customer will give you high marks for things you never knew you were doing well. Confused? Read those sentences again.

A Personal View of the Power of Perception, Not Reality

Many people have a strange image of Oregon. Most mispronounce the word (It's Oregun, not Oregone) and many think Lewis and Clark are probably still paddling their canoe out there, somewhere.

In 1989, I was invited to a party in Sacramento, California. I was living in Medford, Oregon, teaching marketing at Southern

Oregon State College. A young lady at the party heard I was from Medford and wanted to meet me. She said, "I'm from Connecticut. I've never been west of Pittsburgh, but I must tell you, I love everything about Oregon.

"Charles Osgood, in his daily two-minute radio snippet, told about a man in Medford, Oregon, holding up a Domino's delivery truck. The pizza thief had a pitchfork and bicycle and rode off with four pizzas, yelling, 'Pizza power to the people.'

"Isn't that just like Oregon. You are all so wild and crazy, like frontiersmen. Don't you love being part of the real West?"

I looked down at my Bass Weejun penny loafers, tugged on my Lands' End gabardine slacks, looked through my thick LensSavers glasses, and mustered as much Medford male macho as I could and said (in my best Wyatt Earp imitation), "Damn right, purty lady."

The world loves a cowboy.

View from Main Street

For six years I worked as the vice president of marketing for a relatively small ($60 million) carpet manufacturer. We had 40 salespeople who called on small, independent floor covering stores. It was difficult to figure out exactly what these retailers wanted, since our salespeople defined problems in terms of the last crisis. I could never determine what was a systemic problem (something we did wrong every time, since, in our genius, we had planned it that way) or just a onetime screwup.

Finally, we decided to ask our customers, in a questionnaire (there was a drawing for those who completed the 30 questions), how they defined excellent service, and we asked our salespeople to answer what they thought would be our customers' response for all 30 questions. Our customers and salespeople defined excellent service differently. Stores did not want the product the next day (that's what the salespeople thought they would say); they wanted us to keep our promised ship date 100% of the time. The most common response was, "Sure I'd like everything tomorrow, but that's unrealistic. I want to receive my carpet when you promise. Based on that, I'll tell my customer when I can install the carpet.

If you always ship when you promise, it will never look like I lied to her or don't know what I'm doing."

We had listened naively to our customers (Main Street floor covering retailers) and we changed how we serviced them. We did everything to fulfill our new pledge, "We ship when we promise." Not surprisingly, we won an industry award for service. Many of our customers told other stores of the great service they received from our company. Our sales and profits dramatically improved. It never would have happened if we hadn't turned to our customers and taken their direction!

Tom Peters, who first articulated the listen naively idea in a video, tells the story of De Mar, a heating and air-conditioning company in Clovis, California. De Mar does not charge time and a half for service on weekends and nights. Owner Larry Harmon realized time and a half was an industry standard that had nothing to do with his customers' lifestyle or expectations. His customers had complained of this many times. So he decided his organization would reflect his customers' perception of fair price and good service, not how the industry had defined service and pricing. Now he offers one price, anytime, and a discount for senior citizens, anytime. He earns more money than his competition and has created such loyal customers they've become advocates. No new technology, no advertising gimmick, just smart marketing and listening to your customers and believing they know best.

Ashland, Oregon, is a very small town (15,000 population) just north of the California border. It is famous for excellent regional theater, the Oregon Shakespeare Festival. It is also a college town (Southern Oregon State College) and is inhabited by retro, middle-age hippies. Most are Californians who have traded in their BMWs and concrete for a fat-free, guilt-free, morally superior and decidedly less materialistic existence.

Mike Uhtoff left his job as director of the Audubon Society in Portland, Oregon, and moved his family to this "yuppie-gone-rural" enclave. He had no business background, but he did have a full beard, so he decided to open the Northwest Nature Shop in an old, two-story home, just two blocks away from the Shakespeare Festival theaters. (He and his family lived upstairs.) This store had a little bit of everything. It was the quintessential politically correct store. Educational toys, books about the area, specialty topographic maps, cassette tapes of babbling brooks, birdhouses, rocks of all sizes . . . you get the picture. It was delicatessen marketing at its worst, but there was method to this silliness.

Mike started his business with products he liked. He did not know this area, nor did he know who his core customers were or what they wanted from his store. So he started his store as an expensive research project and an ongoing retail operation at the same time. I would not recommend this "let's build the airplane while in flight" approach, but Mike was smart enough and determined that his customers would show him the way.

Mike and his wife, Kathy, listened to their customers, every day, all the time. This was a conscious effort to solicit customer feelings about the store. They had a simple tally sheet of customer recommendations. They asked more than 75% of all customers where they lived and what products they would like to see carried. Every idea and every product was recorded. Each week, Kathy organized the information by customer address.

The locals wanted birdhouses, birdbaths, birdseed, binoculars, and an expanded line of educational toys. Northwest Nature Shop has become the bird-watcher's headquarters with a board for bird-watchers to note when and where they have seen a specific, unique bird. They have regular bird-related classes after store hours. This really is the ultimate listen naively store.

Today, Northwest Nature Shop practices narrowcasting. Mike and Kathy got to that point by listening to their customers, not occasionally, but all the time. Their product assortment and classes reflect exactly what the core customers want. And they continue to listen naively.

GETTING DOWN TO BUSINESS

Applying Marketing Principles to Your Business

MARKETING PRINCIPLE 8
The customer's perception of reality *is* reality. To know what the customer's perception is, the marketer must "listen naively."

1. Do you sit down with 10 customers on a monthly basis and talk about their perception of your business? If not, why?

   _____

   _____

2. Do you have a suggestion box? If not, why? _____

   _____

3. When you send thank-you cards, do you include a self-addressed card the customer may use to grade your store and give suggestions for improvement? If not, why? _____

   _____

4. Do you send out a questionnaire once a year asking your customers to help you improve your business? If not, why?

   _____

   _____

5. List three other methods that you can utilize on a regular basis to listen naively.

   a. _____

   b. _____

   c. _____

MARKETING PRINCIPLE 9

9.
Marketing is a combination of art (feel for what the customer wants) and science (math and analysis) to confirm your artistry. As such, marketing is intensely analytical.

Customers' buying behavior can be found in your monthly marketing reports. These reports tell you about your customers, what they think about you, what they like about you, and what they do not like. This is where you find your core products, core price points, and so on.

Sadly, most stores find it difficult to compile accounting information on a quarterly basis, much less a monthly basis, so the thought of having an entirely different reporting and evaluation system to gather marketing information is foreign to most retailers. It should not be.

I know you have read plenty about the geniuses in the direct-marketing business, but they have grown at twice the rate of regular retail for the last 15 years and one of the reasons is that successful direct-marketing companies follow the numbers. They are intensely analytical.

The successful direct-marketing company knows what the customers buy, how they pay for it, how often they buy, whether it was on promotion, whether they buy compatible items, where they live, and so on. That information has tremendous influence on what products the company will offer in the future, what sales they will run, and how the products will be pictured in their catalog.

The Main Street retailer has the ability (with a computer) to know all the information a direct marketer knows, and then to use the information to make basic marketing decisions for their store. Basic marketing information (sales and profit) should be reviewed at least once a quarter: core products, core price points, broad product markets, and core customers. (See Section I, Marketing, for an explanation of broad product markets and core customers.)

Any computer system that includes a sales, inventory, and

accounting package can do the reporting work in minutes. You just have to ask it.

L.L. Bean—Studying the Numbers

Have you ever thought your customer base was changing, but you weren't sure? Has a new group of customers found you, and you're not quite sure what to do?

In 1968, L.L. Bean, the famous catalog for serious fishermen and hunters, found itself in this happy predicament.

In 1912, L.L. Bean issued its first catalog—one page and one product, the Maine Hunting Shoe. For the next 55 years, L.L. Bean (the owner) directed the company's product mix and advertising toward fishermen and hunters living in the Northeast. It advertised in *Sports Afield, Outdoor Life, Field and Stream,* and *True (Magazine For Men).*

By 1967, L.L. Bean's volume was only $4.6 million, with 300,000 (3-by-5) cards serving as the system for customer (database) information. L.L. Bean only knew who had placed an order, that is, if it could find the right card. L.L. Bean made no attempt to determine from which catalog customers ordered, what they ordered, or how they paid.

In 1968, L.L. Bean asked his son to join the company. A cursory look at their database showed a large percentage of customers were from metropolitan addresses (generally not the location of serious fishermen) and fully one-third were "Mrs." Based on that simple analysis, the company decided to advertise in different magazines and track the results. In three months, *New Yorker* became the Number 1 magazine for customers requesting the catalog and Number 1 in customer dollar purchases. In other words, the *New Yorker* reader requested the catalog, and upon receipt, immediately ordered gear.

L.L. Bean's original core customers (serious fishermen and hunters) were less significant and a new, much more powerful core customer was emerging. Look at the sales in Figure 6-6.

Baby boomers living in metropolitan areas were buying the mystique of L.L. Bean for their own form of urban hardship. Their idea of roughing it was to wear Maine hunting shoes to work when

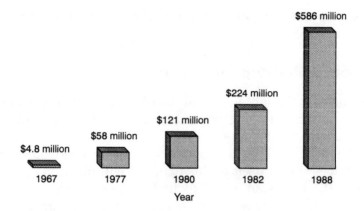

Figure 6-6. L.L. Bean sales 1967–1988. (Source: Annual Reports, L.L. Bean Co.)

it rained or when they took the kids sledding. Fishing or hunting? No way!

Without analysis, L.L. Bean never would have understood these new core customers and the benefits they were seeking. Certainly, it would not be a $700 million company in 1993, with 55% of its products sold to women!

Did L.L. Bean continue to manage its customer list with 3-by-5 cards? Truth be known, the old man fought computerization or using stock numbers for products for some time. Youth prevailed. L.L. Bean built a bonfire and burned 420,000 3-by-5 cards.

Today, L.L. Bean has maintained their old core customers and new urban core customers by using different catalogs. Basically the same items are carried in the different catalogs, but each catalog has expanded choices in their core items, like more hunting boots and sizes for the serious outdoorsmen, and more turtlenecks for the Internet hunter. The analysis of the right customer for the right catalog makes this work.

View from Main Street

Most of the Main Street retailers I know think they are quite good at the art of retail. They think they have a good feel for what the customer wants and could care less about the science of retailing. The popular refrain is, "I've got it all in my head and I know my customer. That statistical analysis is for big companies, who couldn't find their. . . ." That is the small business cop-out and assures mediocrity. In many cases, what made the big companies big was the commitment to knowing the customers better and using the computer to keep track of and in touch with the customers. The successful Main Street retailers I have mentioned in this book, John Norris of Norris Shoes, Dee West of Gary West Meats, and Mike and Kathy Uhtoff of Northwest Nature Shop, would not be as successful if they had relied just on their artistry.

The trouble is when you decide to get serious about the science of retail, a strange cycle begins. You buy a computer and struggle to organize the accounting information—and you curse the day you purchased the computer until you realize you can't live without it. But you still aren't using this technology to make marketing decisions; you've become your own accountant. So the accountant decides to give you marketing advice to justify his monthly fee. If you take it, you curse the day you let the accountant give you marketing advice. The strange cycle continues. (It's hard to know what's worse, a store without a computer or a CPA giving marketing advice.)

A computer and a commitment to the science of retail are strategic necessities. You must have a computer, and it must give you accounting and marketing information. Marketing information—real numbers about your store sales, inventory, and profit—must be part of your quarterly review of your business, and I don't mean a roundtable discussion with your employees about "feelings."

Abbey Carpet Showcase of Largo, Florida, decided to move to a larger store on the busiest street in town. Owner Art Munjone was simply going to transfer his carpet samples, buy some additional products that he liked, and keep on selling. Art had a computer that generated his financial statements, but he did not use it to make marketing decisions. He knew what he liked to sell, and what suppliers he liked, so that was that. His business had grown phenomenally, but his gross profit was less than he desired.

I persuaded Art to analyze his last six months of sales and to remerchandise his entire store if the numbers suggested it. Did they ever! What Art displayed and what he sold were two different things. He *showed* very few Berber-style carpets and *sold* a large amount; he showed a tremendous amount of "fine, formal carpet" and sold little; and his offerings by price point were far out of line. Figure 6-7 shows you sales by price point.

Art learned from this graph that his best-selling price point ($17.99) was his most expensive price point. In other words, he offered only one or two items, out of 86 products, that were more expensive than $17.99. This was a serious marketing error, and contributed to his low gross profit. Unwittingly, Art had established a price ceiling that was considerably lower than the customers wanted.

Your best-selling price point should never be the most expensive or least expensive, but it should be in the middle so customers can trade up or down from the most popular price based on what other benefits they are seeking.

Based on this analysis, Art added 14 Berber carpets and 20 products that were priced over $17.99, and junked all those fine, formal carpets. He improved his gross profit, improved his closing rate (fewer people left to shop at another store), and started selling more expensive carpets. His core customers are much happier with his store.

Art Munjone is one of the best retailers I know, but he found himself responding to manufacturer reps and not core customers.

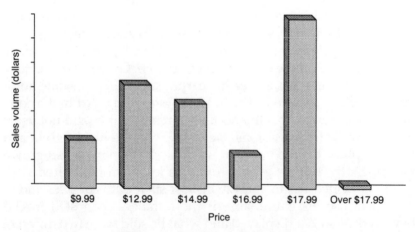

Figure 6-7. Carpet sales by price.

All of a sudden, he had the wrong mix of products. Today, on a quarterly basis, Art reviews his sales and carpet samples and inventory. He'll keep more customers this way.

As I mentioned earlier, Waldenbooks rewards its core customers with an additional discount at point of sale and after they spend $100 they receive a $5 coupon toward their next purchase. It's a good incentive program. A small bookstore in upstate New York (it did not want to be identified) took the Waldenbooks program, matched it discount for discount, coupon for coupon, and then used their database (customer file) information to personalize their relationship with core customers.

This bookstore found that customers tend to read books in one or two fields or subjects and disregard the rest of the books. A science-fiction reader will continue to read in that field and ignore the introduction of a new mystery. So this Main Street retailer tracked the book purchases of core customers through the incentive program and found an average of 45 heavy users or core customers in each general subject matter. Postcards were sent out once a month to their core customers informing them of two or three books they might enjoy. Each customer received a card customized to their reading habits. Their entire advertising budget was for these postcards.

The computer tracks the sales, identifies the customers' reading preferences, matches them with recently published books, and the ultimate low-technology item—the postcard—communicates with the customer. This is very savvy marketing.

GETTING DOWN TO BUSINESS

Applying Marketing Principles to Your Business

MARKETING PRINCIPLE 9
Marketing is a combination of art (feel for what the customer wants) and science (math and analysis) to confirm your artistry. As such, marketing is intensely analytical.

1. Do you have a customer database?

   _____

2. Have you clustered your customers by where they live?

   _____

   _____

   _____

   _____

3. Do you analyze your best-sellers?

   _____

   _____

   Do you analyze your core price points?

   _____

   _____

   _____

   Do you analyze your core styles?

   _____

   _____

   _____

4. What does the analysis indicate about how you can or should change your assortment?

_____

_____

_____

_____

_____

_____

5. Do you have a reporting system on a monthly or quarterly basis for marketing information?

_____

_____

_____

_____

_____

_____

MARKETING PRINCIPLE 10

10.
The three marketing gems for the 1990s:
Convenience
Dominance
Service

Convenience

In the past, people spent time to save money; today, they spend money to save time. Most people experience what demographers call "poverty of time."

Fifteen years ago, auto dealers owned the lion's share of the auto-repair industry. Lube and oil was the most profitable part. For lube and oil, the customer brought the car in at 8 A.M. and picked it up at 5 P.M. How inconvenient! Along comes Jiffy Lube which understood the customers' growing need for convenience. It offered the same lube and oil change in 10 minutes. Jiffy Lube took the most profitable part of the repair business away from auto dealers, and the auto dealers have yet to get it back. Not surprisingly, auto dealers are now doing fewer and fewer repair jobs since the customer has little loyalty to a dealership they rarely visit.

The Main Street retailer must understand this basic need for convenience. Convenience is being open when customers want. Convenience is going to customers' homes when they want. Convenience is getting the right answer the first time. Convenience is saving customers' time. Convenience is respecting the core customers' lifestyle and making it easy for them to buy.

Those are traditional views of convenience, but there is another related issue. In the customer's mind, convenience means, "You will take care of me after the sale if there is a problem, and it won't take a lot of my time to resolve the complaint." Customers want to know that you offer hassle-free customer service. They want assurance that the defective product will be fixed or replaced quickly at their convenience.

Convenience is an all-consuming part of American lifestyle, and the retailer must reflect this basic customer need.

Dominance

Customers respond to specialization. We like specialty in magazines, doctors, lawyers, TV, and catalogs, and we look to retail merchants for that commitment to a more precise focus. Successful specialty stores like Limited, Gap, Benetton, and Victoria's Secret have that precise focus and are dominant in a narrow market.

Dominance also is part of the customer's visual perception. Think of bed-and-bath presentations at a department store. The Laura Ashley rose for bedroom, and some form of that design, will be on bedspreads, pillowcases, sheets, decorator pillows, wallpaper, shams, quilts, draperies, curtains, rugs, lamp shades, and more. No one buys all those roses—just the thought of it would give them hives—but the impact and the dominance of the presentation says: "We know how to put together a singular, unique, total look for your bedroom."

Circuit City has demolished Sears in electronics because it looks and acts like it knows more about electronics. Take TVs, for example. Sears always had a "good," "better," and "best" in three varieties, and that was it. It still sold $400 million worth of TVs. But when you walk into a Circuit City, you see 300 TVs on the same station, 600 eyes looking right and left. Talk about a dominant display. Who appears to be the one that understands and knows TVs better? Circuit City.

The growth of auto malls also is a response to the theory of dominance. Five or six auto dealers create a mall just for autos. Customers are happy that they can shop many different brands in one location. All dealers compete equally: They're open the same time, have the same location, and feed off each other's advertising and promotions.

The largest auto mall in California, Roseville Auto Mall, has gone even further than most. For the first two years, each dealer advertised on their own. The dealers spent only 15% of their advertising on joint "come to the mall" advertising. They decided to capitalize on the value of the mall—dominance and convenience.

Each dealer committed 50% of their advertising to jointly advertise the tremendous assortment of cars, and the convenience to see everything in one auto mall. The commercials were as corny as ever ("Used car blowout," "Best buy of the month," "We're open to midnight," etc.), but the number of TV spots they could buy as a group was so high they dominated the airwaves. Sales skyrocketed and the dealers' advertising cost decreased.

Dominance in retail marketing means the sum of the parts working together exceeds the sum of all the individual parts. Dominance starts with narrowcasting.

Service

Service is the hidden gem. In a computerized, dehumanized society, service is the ticket to success for your Main Street store. More customers are looking for increased value and service increases the value of the product. But you must offer the service the core customer wants, and you must be able to deliver it better than your competition.

Too many retailers resign themselves to giving adequate service; too few commit to excellent service. The difference in cost is pennies and yet it's the margin between success and failure. Don't be penny-wise and pound foolish. (Improving your service quotient will be covered in Section IV, Keeping Customers.)

View from Main Street

Convenience

Main Street retail has responded to the customer's need for convenience. A whole new industry has been spawned—the convenience industry—and almost all of it has been captured by the Main Street retailer. The large company often did not see a change in customer need for convenience (10-minute lube shops, on-site portable lube businesses, at-home lawn-mower repair, etc.) or simply could not figure out how to satisfy the customer's needs and still make a profit. It takes listening naively and hard work. The Main Street retailer could, did, and will continue to find new profit opportunities in the convenience industry.

Far too often, Main Street retailers get comfortable with their store's operation and make only small changes, nothing too disruptive. They forget what got them there, risk taking. Their business methods became one of risk aversion, instead of constant reevaluation and risk taking based on customers' wishes. Much of the convenience industry has come from start-ups, not existing businesses that could have easily expanded and capitalized on this new customer direction, if only they had been listening!

I can't verify this story, but a friend of mine from Lebanon, Pennsylvania, swears it is true. A video-rental store was located on a good road (the busiest street between town and the largest suburban enclave), but the owner wasn't getting the sales she had expected from potential customers who lived in the area. In one month, she talked to 100 potential customers who were not renting videos from her store and she was stunned to learn the reason: She was on the wrong side of the street. Many people, especially women, did not want the hassle of turning left from one of those fifth "suicide" lanes (on their way home) to rent a video. She moved the store across the street but kept a drop-off box in the original location so customers did not have to turn left while going to work. She changed the name of the store to <u>Right Turn</u> Video, and tripled her sales the first year.

That's the ultimate response to customers' desire for convenience.

Dominance

Dominance is rejecting delicatessen marketing and committing to narrowcasting. It's having fewer product types, but a greater assortment and inventory of more brands, colors, and sizes for the product types carried.

Many Main Street retailers experience a conflict between narrowcasting/dominance and giving the customer more convenience by adding a new product line. How should the retailer resolve this marketing conflict? If you can't justify the dollar investment to make a dominant offering of the new product line, don't offer it until you can.

Norris Shoes faced that problem by bringing in a shoe-repair business rather than start its own. Very smart. What Norris didn't do was offer to repair shoes and run the shoes across the street to the repair store. As far as his customers were concerned, he got into the repair business in a dominant, professional way.

Get real or don't get in. That's narrowcasting and dominance.

Service

With the extraordinary growth of the service industry, you would think that service in the retail sector would improve. It has not. Service is the Achilles' heel of the entire retail industry. Overall, Main Street retailers and multichain operations fail at service. The specific failings might vary, but the result is the same—customers are unhappy with the level of service they receive.

Most of the large retailers we shopped and discussed in Chapter 2, The Loud Revolution, try to have as few employees as possible working at any given time. Their motto is, "Keep the cost down." How do you suppose they do that? By keeping a tight rein on floor coverage. Large retailers have essentially lowered the customers' expectations for any human contact or personal service and replaced that with technology service. The most visible, new technology service is, "If you have a Touch-Tone phone, press 1 for. . . ." With each punch of a number, you get closer to the subject or department you want. I call that technology torture.

The Main Street retailer must do much better than that.

Nordstromize your service. That takes commitment, discipline, and an understanding of how the small personal touches make a big difference. (I will cover in detail a plan to improve customer service in Section IV, Keeping Customers.)

The following successful Main Street retailers know the importance of small personal touches:

Winans Furniture, Medford, Oregon

Winans never met a customer complaint it didn't like. When a female customer complains, she receives one red rose with a note promising to resolve the problem. (Remember, a customer offended, then loved and given attention, is an advocate for life.)

Mizell Floors, Valdosta, Georgia

The carpet installers for Mizell carry small cans of white and off-white paint to cover any chips on baseboards they might have made during carpet installation. Customers would only see these chips if they crawled around the floor, but boy are they impressed.

Burgundy Rose, Roseville, California

The Burgundy Rose offers its own 30-day credit account for core customers. Guess what? A very large part of Burgundy Rose business is local telephone orders. (I'm convinced it receives a large share of the unplanned "whim" purchases of flowers from guilt-ridden or love-struck men in search of their better selves.)

Abbey Carpet Co., Sacramento, California

As president of this 450-store franchise, I did not screen my phone calls. All calls came directly to me from the receptionist. (Supposedly, Nordstrom does not allow the management to screen calls. If it's good enough for Nordstrom, anybody should do it.)

Saturn, the subsidiary of GM

I know Saturn is not your mom-and-pop retailer, but my friends who own a Saturn swear that the commercials *aren't* even as good as the real service you get from a Saturn dealer. Now that's a switch—a company whose advertising underpromises. Saturn sells cars the way the customer would like to buy them, and then gives exceptional after-sale service, not the regular haphazard auto-dealer service.

Sadly, most Main Street retailers give more lip service than real service. For them, service is intangible and hard to measure. To me, good service is the easiest and most tangible way for the Main Street retailer to be different. A major part of Section IV, Keeping Customers, will be devoted to improving your overall customer service.

1. List six ways in which you are more convenient to your customers than your competition.

    a. _____

    b. _____

    c. _____

    d. _____

    e. _____

    f. _____

2. For the type of products you sell, do you have dominant presentations that convince people you really understand that business better than the competition?

    _____

    _____

3. For a growing product segment, do you have a dominant presentation that indicates you have a great assortment of this new look?

    _____

    _____

4. List the different services you offer to your customer.

    _____

    _____

    _____

_____

_____

5. List four additional services you could offer your customers
    that would benefit them and increase the value to them.

    a. _____

    b. _____

    c. _____

    d. _____

MARKETING PRINCIPLE 11

11.
It is always more believable to market value than price.

Figure 6-8 shows the value equation for a retailer.
There are two ways to increase the value of a product.

1. Keep the benefits delivered to the customer the same as your competition, and reduce the price (Figure 6-9).
2. Keep the price the same as your competition, but increase the benefits delivered to the customer (Figure 6-10).

If you do not always want to be the low-price leader, Option 2—increase the benefits—is the way to go.

This equation restates many of the marketing principles you have reviewed.

Value is always more lasting and believable than price. I believe it is easier to create and defend an identity that is based on more and better customer benefits than on price alone.

But if you offer the same benefits to your core customers as your competition, then price becomes all-consuming.

You must offer more and better benefits to your key customers for the price issue to diminish and the value to increase.

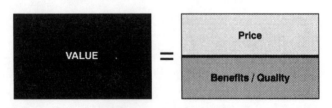

Figure 6-8. Value equation.

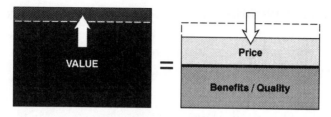

Figure 6-9. Increase value by reducing price.

Increased Importance of Price

Price and service have become more important in the 1990s than ever before. Customers are looking for lower prices *and* better service, which is not easy to deliver.

Low-price promises are growing in all retail segments, as you saw in my competitive analysis (Trivers retail meter) in Chapter 2, The Loud Revolution. There were 73 warehouse clubs (Price Club, Costco, etc.) in 1985; by mid-1995, there were 1,000 such clubs. In 1985, Wal-Mart did half the sales volume of Sears. In 1996, it is twice the size of Sears. In 1985, there were three outlet centers (Freeport, Maine; Morristown, New Jersey; Reading, Pennsylvania) in the United States. By 1996, there are 82 major outlet centers and 400 smaller outlet malls.

Let me state the price/value issue again. The Main Street retailer has these choices:

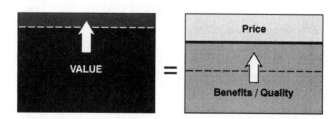

Figure 6-10. Increase value by improving benefits.

Offer a lower price, but the same benefits and services as the competition.

Offer the same price, but more benefits and services than the competition.

About 99% of all Main Street retailers sell similar products and brands that are virtually indistinguishable. I don't care what the manufacturer rep says, the stuff looks the same, certainly in the customer's mind. (If you are among the 1% who is lucky enough to sell a group of products that everyone wants, but no other retailer has, forget this principle. You already have the value story.) Product or brand alone will not increase your value quotient. You have to look outside the product to increase the value of your store: better warranty; more appealing display; more convenient hours of operation; wider assortment; deeper inventory; better-trained salespeople; and most importantly, better customer service.

The successful Main Street retail store cannot offer adequate benefits (the same as everyone else) and adequate prices. You must increase the number of and raise the quality of benefits the core customer wants. You do that by listening naively to your core customer.

A Personal View of Value and Price

When we moved to Medford, Oregon, in 1983, the only stores that resembled larger department stores were a small Sears and Lamonts (part of a regional chain) that carried clothing and bed-and-bath ensembles. My wife saw a jacket that I needed for the upcoming damp winter and suggested I buy it at Lamonts. I did. I paid full retail. My wife said, "You'll be the best-dressed outdoorsman in Medford."

For the next 60 days, I never saw my jacket around town. I was the sole owner of this stylish coat. Then I started to see men wearing the jacket and within the next 60 days many were wearing it. I visited the Lamonts manager and asked him about the sales of my jacket. He said, "In our first promotion, which was half price, we sold 38 coats; then three weeks later we gave an additional 20% off the half price and we sold 74; finally, last Saturday we sold 96 coats for $25. And you know, one dumb schmo paid regular price."

View from Main Street

The newspaper ad in Figure 6-11 ran in selected markets on the West Coast in August 1995.

Finally, Green's has come to grips with their value story. Green's was going down a bottomless "low price" pit as it fought the price war. Green's belatedly recognized that superior service was their real strength, and introduced the "nickel difference."

I love the nickel difference story. You can be sure Green's built their reputation on superior customer service. The benefits it lists are the core customer benefits. Their future is tied to these benefits and finding more customers like their core customers. I bet Green's succeeds.

GETTING DOWN TO BUSINESS

Applying Marketing Principles to Your Business

MARKETING PRINCIPLE 11
It is always more believable to market value than price.

1. If you do not want to be the price leader in the marketplace, what are the additional benefits that improve the value of your store to customers?

   _____

   _____

2. Do you think your customers know that you offer these benefits?

   _____

   _____

NO MORE WAR

THE WAR IS FINALLY OVER.

You've seen the price war going on for years. We lower our prices, then the Mega Stores lower theirs. Well, say "**No more price war.**" Our vacuum cleaners, sewing machines and sergers will always be 1 nickel higher than the prices you'll find advertised by Mega Stores. Since the war is over we can now concentrate on what we do best!

SERVICE

The nickel difference at GREEN'S	GIANT MEGA STORES
20 to 30 times the models and brands available at mega stores.	**NOT**
Operating and demo machines to try.	**NOT**
Trained repair staff on the premises.	**NOT**
Assembly and set-up available.	**NOT**
Instruction available on most products.	**NOT**
Warranty and service station for most brands.	**NOT**
Locally owned and operated so money is recycled in Southern Oregon.	**NOT**
Pull-up and honk for free carry-in service.	**NOT**

Green's
SEWING & VACUUM CENTER

Figure 6-11. A great value statement.

3. Do your core customers think these are the best benefits to improve the value of your business in their minds?

_____

_____

MARKETING PRINCIPLE 12

12.
Loyalty ladder revisited. To climb the loyalty ladder, the retailer must exceed the customer's expectations.

Let's go back to the loyalty ladder. It's not easy to transform customers into clients and advocates. It won't happen because you are nice.

I have participated in many customer-satisfaction surveys. Most produce the customer ratings shown in Figure 6-12.

Management was always ecstatic; 85% of the customers were satisfied or felt service was superior. But the 65% who said the service was satisfactory also said they saw no difference between our company and the competition. In other words, they would buy from the competitor if it gave them a reason to do so. There was no reason to become a client at my company.

"Satisfactory" or "adequate" is the worst reputation you can have. If that's the best the customer can say about you, you did not make a lasting impression. That's not satisfactory for your business, is it?

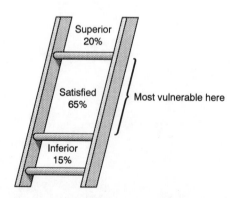

Figure 6-12. Customer satisfaction survey.

To climb the loyalty ladder (Figure 6-13), the retailer must exceed customer expectations.

In most cases, the Main Street retailer can exceed customer expectations with better service during and after the sale. Think of service in broad terms. I'll bet there are five additional services you could include in your business that would improve the value of the products you are selling and cost little to implement. Remember, the cost you want to avoid is the cost of losing a customer to your competitor.

At Marriott Hotels, Bill Marriott says people don't return because of the "atrium with skylights," they come back because the misplaced shirt was sent home and rooms have a small coffeemaker. Extra service. Extra value. That's what keeping customers and creating clients and advocates is all about.

A Personal View of How *Not* to Build Loyalty

My wife, Karen, and I decided to take the family to a new ice-cream parlor in Wheaton, Illinois. It was 1978, but the Trivers family was no Brady Bunch; it was very difficult to persuade all five children, ages 4 to 15, to do anything together, and if we did, what actually happened in a public place was anybody's guess, and my continued embarrassment.

Figure 6-13. Customer loyalty ladder.

Nathan, the youngest, was allowed to order first. He ordered a double scoop. Not to be outdone or somehow cheated, Conor, 7, ordered a triple and so on. After the new employee had completed three orders, and right before she was going to give them to the three youngest of our clan, the owner asked the employee if she had weighed the cones to be sure they weren't too large. She had not. She dutifully weighed each cone and shaved off ice cream to ensure each cone was within the weight standards—all this in the name of cost control.

So here's the scene: Three children (age 4, 7, and 8), their faces pressed against the glass, watched their ice-cream cones reduce in size for no apparent reason. Conor, the moral equivalent to Mother Teresa for the protection of large ice-cream cones, asked the employee why she would willingly and openly cheat children who were spending their allowance for ice cream. (It was not his allowance money.) Robert, a future businessman, came around the counter brandishing an ice-cream scoop; he told the employee that he would replace twice the amount that was being stolen from his brothers. Nathan sat down and cried. Kelly, our daughter, informed the owner that her entire junior high school class was going to picket this store for 10 years, and John Michael, the only one with common sense, left, vowing never to participate in another family outing until the twenty-first century.

Some of you might be disheartened about the behavior of our children. I agree. But the owner's behavior, although understandable, was wrong. It is one thing for a deli to weigh the meat or cheese since it is sold by the pound, but to weigh an ice-cream cone (when the cost and portion-control instrument is the scoop) is silly and offensive.

Remember, to be cost conscious at the expense of being customer conscious is a terrible mistake.

View from Main Street

The goal of all businesses is to find and keep customers. The better you serve them, the more loyal they will be. The more loyal they are, the more they will actively advocate your business. The more advocates you have, the more you'll find similar core customers.

The more you build your core-customer base, the better you'll serve their needs. You create a cycle of marketing success.

Russ Hoover of Fairfield, California, understands and appreciates the value of creating advocates, and how they help in finding more customers like themselves. His Gillespie's Carpet Center sends out a thank-you note to every customer who has floor covering installed in their home. Inside is a prestamped questionnaire asking the customers to evaluate the service. At the end of the questionnaire, Gillespie's asks if the customer would recommend Gillespie's, and, if so, could their name be used.

Mrs. Jenkins (not her real name) was very happy with the service and wrote that Gillespie's could use her name. An appointment was made to photograph the new carpet and obtain a quote from her. She said, "The installers were so professional, I didn't even have to have my grand piano tuned." Wow! The installers moved the piano out of the living room, installed the carpet, and moved the piano back, and were so gentle that Mrs. Jenkins, a piano teacher, did not have to have the piano retuned! She read the statement for a radio commercial.

All the creative advertising in the world is not as potent as a satisfied customer singing your praises to the heavens. Mrs. Jenkins didn't just convince other piano teachers that Gillespie's had a special concern for customers. Many consumers like Mrs. Jenkins connected with her message. It wasn't price, speed of delivery, or freebies, it was attention to the details of excellent service, all spoken in the idiom of a satisfied customer.

Excellent service is not doing one big thing well. It is the sum of doing many small tasks well, the very tasks your core customers are looking for. In a country where technology has replaced real customer service, excellent service is so rare that it always exceeds the customer's expectations and creates advocates. Every time!

GETTING DOWN TO BUSINESS

Applying Marketing Principles to Your Business

MARKETING PRINCIPLE 12
Loyalty ladder revisited. To climb the loyalty ladder, the retailer must exceed the customer's expectations.

1. In what ways do you exceed the customer's expectations?

    _____

    _____

    _____

2. If you believe your store gives excellent customer service, list 10 things that always occur with every customer contact.

    a. _____

    b. _____

    c. _____

    d. _____

    e. _____

    f. _____

    g. _____

    h. _____

    i. _____

    j. _____

3. How do you know that the core customers think these 10 "excellent service" items are the ones they want and expect from your company?

    _____

7

A MARKETING SUCCESS STORY

February 1985—Medford, Oregon

Kathy, an aspiring young entrepreneur, decided to open a soft-yogurt store. Her brother had told her that they were popping up all over the San Francisco area and that they were a great hit.

The first thing Kathy did was ask her professors where she should open this store. She received two answers: the large regional mall or in Ashland, Oregon. Ashland is a "granola" town where people worry about the feelings of asparagus. As it turned out, neither of the professors' answers was correct. That, in itself, was an important lesson: Never ask professors about something practical. With that bit of misinformation, she decided to complete some street-savvy market research. She visited 48 soft-yogurt stores in the San Francisco area. Some store owners were reluctant to talk. On those occasions, she even went through their garbage to see if she could find where they purchased certain items. She talked to 800 customers. She knew who the largest core-customer group was and what benefits they sought from soft yogurt: The core customer was a working woman who wanted a light lunch or light snack.

Kathy built her entire marketing and business strategy around the core customer and the benefits she was seeking. The Yogurt Grove was located in downtown Medford, within walking distance of where the largest percentage of working women were employed. The interior was very bright, decorated in purple and green colors.

The tables were round and the chairs were wood. The sizes of yogurt she offered were tiny, small, and medium (men generally lie about things that have to do with size and naturally would have named their sizes big, gigantic, and megaworld). She was right on target. If you are serving something that is supposed to be light and low-calorie, the name of the size should imply that fact.

When dispensing a tiny portion, employees had been trained in a special kind of gyrating wrist action that made the yogurt curl around and around and it appeared that the customer was getting more than what was ordered. Even people who order "tiny" love to get more than they paid for.

Everything about Yogurt Grove was feminine. Everything was directed at the core customer, and it was a fabulous success.

Twelve days after it opened, a man walked in at lunch and looked around at 43 working women sitting at small round tables in this well-lit, warm, and feminine yogurt shop. He asked an employee, "Can I be here?"

III

FINDING CUSTOMERS

8

FINDING CUSTOMERS: THE THREE STEPS

If you're smiling, you're not working, because no one said retail was funny.

It's time to stop smiling and do the necessary, but un-fun work of finding customers.

The principles of marketing work only if you "know how to know" your customer. Without the real, empirical knowledge of who your key customers are, where they live, and what they buy, you only will "pretty much, kinda" know and it won't be very accurate, anyhow.

Marketing principles make sense and can help your company if you commit to the un-fun work of knowing the core of your business. Remember the phrase, "Spectacular business success is always preceded by unspectacular preparation"? Most Main Street retailers avoid, at all cost, the drudgery of unspectacular preparation. Many would rather schmooze the banker than prepare a business plan. Many would rather create the great ad that will knock 'em dead than segment their customer base. Many would rather risk inventory dollars on a hot, new item to make the season a success than build a complete customer-service program. But without the real knowledge of your core and secondary customers, your Main Street retail store will always be firmly planted in midair. That might be fun, but it's not very smart, nor is it good for your company.

You have been forewarned. Don't read any further without a pencil (with ample eraser) and your best business mind. But it's okay to smile.

RETAIL STORES WITH DOORS AND PATHWAYS

Businesses fail not because they run out of money, but because they run out of customers. Businesses fail because they don't know how to find and keep customers.

In the past 10 years, the intensity and quantity of new retail and nonretail (catalog marketing) competition have played havoc on the existing Main Street retailers. Never before in retail history have so many new forms of competition moved into Anywhere, U.S.A., seemingly at the same time. These new competitors recognized one simple marketing fact: They had to steal some of your customers to build their business. Likewise, you had to hold on to your core customers to stay in business.

If you want to win the continuing tug-of-war for customers, you must know who your core and secondary customers are. Then, and only then, will you win the battle and continue to prosper.

You will prosper when you find new customers, but not just any new customers. You need to find new customers who are like your best existing customers. Again, we come to the catch-22: You can't find (you can, it's just so expensive and wasteful) the right new customers unless you know who your core customers are, and what benefits and products they seek from your Main Street retail store.

Finding customers is broken down into three parts:

1. Markets
2. Segmenting markets
3. Building markets and creating benefits.

In this section, Finding Customers, you will learn how to complete these four important tasks without the expense of research departments and legions of consultants.

Finding customers is not just about advertising, it is about knowing the customer groups that buy from you and knowing who your core customers are and what they buy so you can find more customers like them.

If you are to succeed in marketing, all marketing tactics (advertising, promotions, etc.) must follow the basic steps of finding customers: Define the markets you serve, segment (break into smaller groups) your markets, build the best markets for your store, and create benefits that your core customer is seeking. Now you're ready to advertise and promote. You'll get more from these marketing investments than ever before.

So that you will know how to apply the concepts of segmenting, building markets, and creating benefits, I have used a floor-covering specialty store, Trivia Carpets by Trivers, as an example. To help visualize these marketing concepts, I have used the metaphor of different doors (into the store) and different pathways to the doors. In a general sense, doors are "broad product markets" you participate in, and pathways are different "customer groups." Doors are like a group of departments in a big store, and pathways are the customers who buy from those departments.

To be a marketing retailer, think of your store with at least three or four doors (broad markets or departments), and many pathways (different customer groups or submarkets) leading to the doors. You want to know as much as possible about the customers coming along the pathways and entering the different doors.

Doors and pathways—it's a key marketing concept.

Trivia Carpets by Trivers

Let's take a look at Trivia Carpets by Trivers and see how marketing wise the company is.

Presently, Trivia Carpets by Trivers (Figure 8-1) is an un-marketing company. That's not to say Trivia Carpets hasn't been pretty successful; it has. In 14 months, Home Depot is opening up, and a regional look-alike to Home Depot is

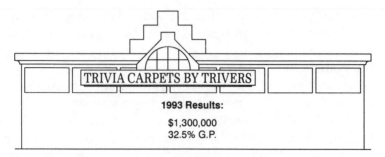

Figure 8-1. The un-marketing company.

expanding into floor covering. To add insult to injury, two of Trivers's best installers have decided to start their own floor-covering store. They think if someone as disorganized as Trivers can succeed in this business, they can, too. The ingrates. (Whether we like it or not, that's how and why most businesses start. That's why Trivers did.)

So, Trivers is rethinking his market position, where he gets his business, and what type of business he's in. He has feelings about this, but that's all they are—feelings. The only real information Trivers has is what the accountant reported as his 1994 financial results. The banker will find it helpful and so will the IRS, but it is of no use for Trivers's marketing planning.

Trivers used to exhort his salespeople with, "Treat the customers right. Give them what they want." Never did any of this training suggest that different customers were buying from different departments seeking different benefits. In this state of marketing (customer) ignorance, Trivers knew nothing about his customers.

In Section III, Finding Customers, we'll follow this stubbornly proud, "I'd rather seek forgiveness than ask for approval" entrepreneur. By describing and analyzing Trivia Carpets by Trivers in terms of doors (broad product markets or separate businesses) and pathways (different customer groups), Trivers will be prepared for Home Depot and any other retailer silly enough to take him on!

9

MARKETS: UNDERSTANDING YOUR DIFFERENT CUSTOMERS

DEFINITION

A market is a group of customers with some common life characteristics and similar product and store preferences.

To be a market, the group of customers must be unique (different from other groups in three or four ways that affect their buying habits) and substantial (large enough to merit a marketing effort).

You have heard, "Is there a market for the product?" or, "If I could just find my market." The word "market" is used in so many different ways, it's important to understand fully the most helpful definition: Markets are unique customer groups with unique buying habits. Your business has different markets (customers) that buy your products for different reasons. Unique customer groups use different pathways to enter your store.

Many retailers research and follow product sales, not customers. That is fine for inventory replenishment and considering new products, but it does not satisfy the basic principle of marketing: Marketing starts with customers. You must know your customers *and* what they buy—doors and pathways. Walk on!

TYPES OF MARKETS

GENERAL MARKETS

Each retailer can sell in two general markets—consumer and/or business.

Every retailer has the potential of selling to two different general markets:

1. *Consumer markets.* Individuals buying products or services for their personal consumption or use.
2. *Business markets.* Businesses buying for their use or redistribution. Examples: when a business buys 10 of your clocks for its use, or when the CEO of the biggest manufacturer in town sets up a gift program through your store for employment anniversaries for all employees with more than five years' service.

Many retailers don't take the business market seriously. That is a mistake. Almost all Main Street retailers have potential sales in the business market, whether they sell cookies, yogurt, gifts, or bicycles. Toys? You bet. Funeral homes? Maybe not.

Obviously, you will need a different marketing approach for business markets, but by separating your store into two large markets, you begin to visualize new opportunities. Then you figure out the best marketing tactics for this different market (different from the consumer market).

Any Main Street retailer should garner at least 20% of their total volume from the business market, with no additional overhead. That's the key. With the same personnel and basic products, but different marketing tactics, you can improve your net profit by selling to the business market.

Take cookies, for instance. The Cookie Connection was a single, independent store located in Medford, Oregon. The cookies were made the way grandma made them: One cookie contained two months' supply of your fat and cholesterol needs. But, boy, were they delicious!

The Cookie Connection, located downtown, marketed to walk-in traffic, but was not breaking even. The owners realized their problem was too much overhead or, stated properly, their bakers and equipment weren't busy enough. They did not feel that more advertising would increase sales enough to offset the expense.

The two partners considered opportunities in the business market. The business market seemed to have big sales potential, if they could make an adequate profit. They brainstormed and came up with ten ideas. Four became winners. These were the doors opened and pathways created in the business section:

- ☐ Fun Friday—supply and deliver 900 cookies every Friday to the local V.A. hospital
- ☐ Retirement homes—became sole supplier of cookies to four retirement homes
- ☐ Birthday cookie—set up a program for three companies to celebrate employee birthdays with special cookie cakes
- ☐ Soccer cookie—set up cookie selling for soccer teams to raise money

Their initial success with the business market energized the owners so much that they continued their search for new doors for the consumer side of their business. Cookiegrams delivered to the home? Naturally! How about a bouquet of cookies for Mother's Day and Valentine's Day? Of course.

Each door opened required different marketing tactics, but used the same product. Sales increased dramatically and so did walk-in traffic, a bonus from selling to the business market. The Cookie Connection delivered cookies to more than 1,200 patients at the local V.A. hospital and retirement facilities. The patients' friends and relatives were introduced to their cookies and many became regular customers.

Trivia Carpets by Trivers

Let's take a look at Trivia Carpets by Trivers (Figure 9-1).
Trivers will divide the store into two parts to signify the two general markets he could or does participate in:

1. Consumer markets
2. Business markets

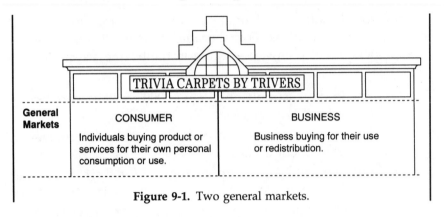

Figure 9-1. Two general markets.

BROAD PRODUCT MARKETS—DOORS

Each general market (consumer and business) has broad product markets or doors. Broad product markets (doors) are smaller, specific, and unique product groups or departments that attract different customers.

Broad product markets are usually defined in terms of the end use of the product. They can be thought of as separate profit centers or departments that have unique marketing characteristics and deliver different sales and profit potential to your store. These broad product markets (doors) are more than the typical departments in a Sears or Nordstrom. A broad product market for Sears would be "Do-it-Yourself Home Improvement," and would include the hardware, paint, and plumbing departments. Installed roofing by a Sears contractor would be part of a different broad product market, "Installed Home Improvement."

Don't despair. "End use of product" may seem confusing, but there are resources (see the end of this chapter) to help you find your doors, which are key to knowing your customers. Remember, the benefits customers seek from each broad product market, and the marketing tactics used to gain their acceptance, are sufficiently different from one broad product market to another.

Trivia Carpets by Trivers

Look at Figure 9-2. With defined broad product markets (doors), this retail store begins to look like a store that understands the makeup of its business and, ultimately, its customers.

Trivia Carpets by Trivers could sell to three distinct broad product markets in the consumer market. Each broad product market (door) has sufficiently different marketing and consumer characteristics. The three broad product markets (doors) are:

1. *Professionally installed floor covering.* The customer buys new carpet (without rake) to replace old, ugly shag (with rake). Trivia Carpets will take care of everything: measure and install the carpet, and take the old carpet away.
2. *Do-it-yourself floor covering.* The customer takes care of everything, including measuring, picking up carpet and installation supplies at the store, and installing the carpet. The old carpet goes in the doghouse.
3. *Professional carpet cleaning.* Store employees professionally clean the carpet.

Now consider how the marketing characteristics and benefits are different for the do-it-yourself department (door) and the professionally installed department (door). The do-it-yourself customers want to take the carpet with them today, and they expect to save money since they will install the carpet. A large assortment is less important than immediate availability and price. They need all the supplies to install the carpet, some training or guidance on how to measure the amount of carpet they will need, and how to complete the installation.

The customers interested in buying professionally installed carpet are looking for a very large selection of carpet, many price points, assurance of professional and timely installation, and warranties for both product and installation. It's a separate door.

Trivia Carpets could sell to four distinct broad product markets in the business market. Each of these broad product markets (doors) has sufficiently different marketing characteristics from the others:

1. *Other businesses.* The business owner buys carpet for their own store or office.

2. *Insurance replacement.* An insurance company buys carpet for a consumer after fire or water damage to the floor. The customer chooses the carpet but the insurance company decides how much to reimburse.

3. *Apartment.* An apartment owner buys carpet for tenant's use.

4. *New home.* The consumer chooses the carpet for their newly constructed home, and the builder decides which products are available and the price. In most cases, price is included in the home's cost.

The benefits the business customer seeks from these four broad product markets are different. The apartment owner orders carpet a few days before it's needed. Ugly's okay . . . but cheap's best. A bank buying carpet for one of its branches is looking for design, color, and wearability. Price is last.

Figure 9-2. Doors define broad product markets.

TARGET MARKETS—PATHWAYS

Important distinct customer groups. Core market is your most important target market.

Each broad product market (door) has at least one, and no more than three, target markets (pathway). More than three distinct customer groups might enter any door, but the three largest will represent more than 80% of the customers and sales. They are your target markets. The largest target market for each broad product market is the core market.

Visualize doors and pathways. Customers who come to a specific door are not alike. Each pathway represents a different, distinct customer group. The largest customer group in number of customers and retail sales volume will have the largest pathway and be your core customer.

PATHWAYS TO DOORS FOR CONSUMERS

Consumer target markets (pathways) are defined by demographic and lifestyle characteristics. This means your customers, who are buying for their own use, should be described as three-dimensional beings, not just as an income bracket. The idea of markets presumes that aspects of our life affect how and what we buy. The more you know about those aspects or characteristics of your target markets, the easier it will be to market to them.

The hard part is to figure out what characteristics are important in the decision-making process for buying from your different broad product markets (doors). For most retailers, the demographic and lifestyle factors to be considered are:

- Sex
- Age
- Income
- Education
- Number of children at home

☐ Marital status

☐ Location of home

☐ Location of employment

I believe sex, age, income, and the location of home are the four factors that impact all buying decisions regardless of product or service. But a customer is more than the sum of these four factors. You will need to consider the nature of your broad product markets (doors) and add one or two other factors I have listed, or others that you think are significant. Those five or six factors will determine how you define your different target markets.

PATHWAYS TO DOORS FOR BUSINESSES

Target markets for business are defined in terms of size and type of operation. Since you are dealing with other businesses (not consumers), you consider how they conduct their business and the specific benefits they are seeking. The key characteristics for determining how many target markets (pathways) you have for each broad business market are:

☐ Who the ultimate product user is

☐ Size of the business

☐ Key benefit you must deliver to the business

The business target markets are often just a few companies that offer the opportunity for considerable sales volume. You are on a first-name basis with the owner. That's good, but tracking your sales and profit, and analyzing the marketing potential of this type of business, remain essential. Don't be lulled by personal relationships, or get a false sense of security with this business. Remember, the bigger the customer, the more dangerous the relationship. How do you dance with a bear? Let the bear lead, don't step on his toes, and don't stop dancing until he does!

Your retail store should be selling to the business market. But you must understand the pitfalls of this marketing and you must know the sales and profit each type of business is generating. The question is: Should you dance with this particular bear?

Trivia Carpets by Trivers

Look at Figure 9-3. The door and pathway analogy has helped Trivers understand his different business segments and the customers who buy from him.

Trivers asked his major suppliers if they had any research relating to consumer buying of floor covering and ancillary services. He determined from those studies and his own intuition that the determining demographic and lifestyle factors that are relevant to his consumer market were:

- ☐ Sex
- ☐ Age
- ☐ Income
- ☐ Number of children at home
- ☐ Location of home

A target market (pathway) could be described in the following manner: 40- to 55-year-old woman, $40,000 household income, two children at home, lives six miles from store. That customer type would represent one pathway.

Another pathway could be older couples: over 50 years old, $60,000+ income, no children at home, live in new development, 14 miles from store.

Don't yawn. This is the way to visualize and understand your business. In Chapter 10, Segmenting Markets, you'll learn how to determine who is on your pathways.

In the business market, Trivia Carpets sells to new-home builders. They represent one door on the business side of his store. Trivers believes he sells to two different types of home builders: custom builders who build no more than 10 homes a year and the tract or volume builder who builds more than 100 homes a year. These two builders are distinct builders in that they seek different benefits from Trivia Carpets, even though the end product is floor covering. Trivers knows this, but he doesn't know the exact sales volume from each type builder and he only has an inkling about the gross profit each generates. Both may be mutually exclusive of each other and Trivers may never be a significant force with either type. He won't come to that marketing wisdom by "kinda knowing"; it will come only from real information and analysis of market potential for these two different types of new-home, floor-covering sales.

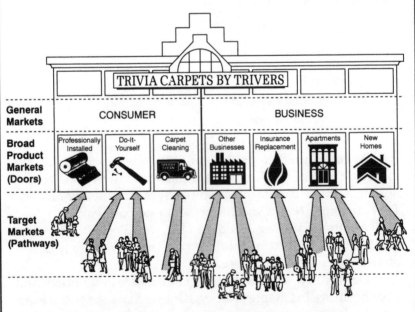

Figure 9-3. Understanding markets: doors and pathways.

Conclusion: Knowing Your Doors and Pathways

Establishing and defining your business in terms of markets is the way to organize and understand the customer (market) components of your business. The more precise the market (customer group), the better your ability to find more of these same types of customers. However, the market must be substantial enough (sufficient volume potential) to warrant a total marketing effort.

The doors and pathways analogy is a simple way to help you visualize and better understand specific markets.

Knowing your different customer groups is essential if you want to find more like them.

There is no right number of broad product markets (doors) and there is no correct list of broad product markets for retailers selling the same goods. Another floor-covering store might have broad markets different from those for Trivia Carpets by Trivers. That's okay.

If you are unsure how to delineate and describe the broad markets for your retail store, you need to:

1. Ask key suppliers to help.
2. Ask the local newspaper advertising representative to help. (Newspapers have excellent resources for many retailers.)
3. Ask your radio and TV stations to help. They also have resources for retailers.
4. If you are near a college or university with a business school, contact it. It probably has a number of classes that emphasize practical application of theory and that would take on your assignment to determine your broad markets (doors).
5. Your local library can help. Most libraries are on line with data/information-retrieval systems. With the proper guidance, they can access articles and statistics about your retail business and the broad markets you are in or should be in.
6. Contact the national retail association that represents your retail store. It compiles data about broad markets for your type of business. (If you don't know the name of the association, your library should have a resource book on all national associations.)

7. Contact your Small Business Development Center. The centers are generally attached to colleges but are supported by the Small Business Administration. They have business counselors on staff. Their advice is free and worth your time. They can be a great resource and information partner for your store.

In the next chapter, you will take the concepts of markets and learn how to find core customers for your store. If you continue to use the simple analogy of doors and pathways, you will see your store the way your customers do.

GETTING DOWN TO BUSINESS

Applying Marketing Principles to Your Business

MARKETS
A market is a group of customers with some common life characteristics and similar product and store preferences.
To be a market, the group of customers must be unique (different from other groups in three or four ways that affect their buying habits) and substantial (large enough to merit a marketing effort).

1. Do you participate in the consumer market? _____

   Do you participate in the business market? _____ If not, why?

   _____

   _____

   _____

2. List the broad product markets for your store.
   Consumer broad product markets (doors):

   a. _____

   b. _____

   c. _____

   d. _____

   Business broad product markets (doors):

   a. _____

   b. _____

   c. _____

3. Are the marketing characteristics different for each broad product market? _____

4. Are the sales and profit potential different? _____

   (The answer must be Yes on questions 3 and 4 for your broad product market to be a legitimate, useful broad product market.)

5. Restate your broad product markets. (Apply simple name for each door.)

   Consumer doors:

   a. _____

   b. _____

c. _____

d. _____

Business doors:

a. _____

b. _____

c. _____

You have taken the first step in understanding your customer.

10

SEGMENTING MARKETS: FINDING YOUR CORE CUSTOMERS

DEFINITION

Segmenting is the process of sorting, organizing, and describing broad product and target markets.

The purpose of segmenting is:

1. To determine the real business value of broad product markets (doors)
2. To find and determine the sales volume of the core target markets (pathways) and at least two smaller target markets

Segmenting is not an academic exercise or something you do when you have time. Segmenting is not only for the big company, it's also for the Main Street retailer who wants to be very profitable. *Knowledge of your customers and profit are synonymous.*

You segment your market (customers) so you can find the key, core target markets (customers) who are most important to your business. Without knowing them, you don't really know the best and least expensive way to communicate with them. When you know your core customer, you have marketing gold!

Segmenting is an intensely analytical method of looking at customers. It requires the discipline of math and absolute belief

149

that statistical data can be transformed into useful marketing information which can be used to make smart marketing decisions.

I have started this chapter with the business general market, which is easier to segment. Let the fun begin.

SEGMENTING STEPS—BUSINESS MARKET

Step 1
Identify broad product markets (doors) in which you are presently selling. Determine volume and profitability.

The segmenting of the business market is a process of refining (reducing) your universe of customers into understandable components or markets. Each refinement focuses the target markets.

Knowing what broad product markets (doors) you sell in and their value is the first step in segmenting the business market. It should not be the last.

How to Compute the Numbers

For planning and goal-setting purposes, each broad product market should be budgeted quarterly for sales and gross profit. Compile this information from sales checks. Regardless of the size of the purchase (cookies to carpet), all sales to the business market should be controlled on a sales check. Simply code each sales check to designate the appropriate broad product market.

Each quarter, add up the sales from sales checks for each broad product market. Based on your cost from supplier or distributor, compute the gross profit, then total.

Trivia Carpets by Trivers

Remember the depiction of Trivia Carpets by Trivers as an un-marketing company? He knew his total sales and gross profit. Now look at Figure 10-1. See how he's beginning to understand and visualize the components of his business.

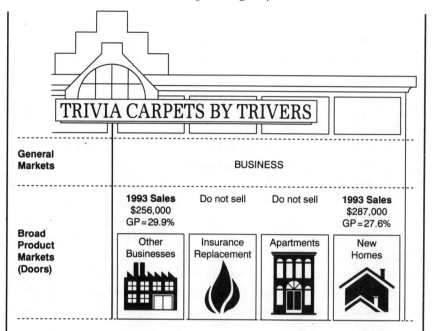

Figure 10-1. The value of the segmented markets.

As you can see, Trivia Carpets is trying to become a marketing-committed retailer. It sells to two broad product markets in the business market and has chosen not to sell to two others. Trivers now knows the dollar volume and gross profit of the two markets he sells, but he does not know the target markets. To make intelligent marketing decisions, he needs to know his pathways.

But look at what he does know. The "new homes" door is the biggest broad market for the business market, but it delivers less gross profit. Does he want to continue to expand this market? Can he improve the gross profit without hurting sales? From the standpoint of time spent, is the marketing cost so great that the lower gross profit makes this business even less profitable?

Now that Trivers has the real numbers, he can begin to answer these and other questions. It's a much better approach than the old SWAG (Scientific Wild Ass Guess) method.

Step 2
Further refine (segment) broad product markets into smaller target markets that have distinct marketing characteristics. Describe and quantify.

or

Find the pathways (target markets) that lead to the doors (broad markets). Describe and quantify.

This is the key step in segmenting business markets. Each pathway (target market) that leads to a door (broad product market) has a different type of business using the pathway. Each target market will respond differently to marketing tactics and product offerings.

Following this process, you will be able to determine the value of the specific, individual customer. This is impossible for consumer markets, since you have many individual customers, but for the business market you should plan to monitor the sales and profit of the separate businesses, the target market, and the broad product market.

How to Compute the Numbers

For planning and goal-setting purposes, budget your sales and gross profit by target market on a quarterly basis. The entire process is very simple. Use the same method you used for broad product markets: Just code the sales checks. (For example, A1—A is a specific broad market, 1 is a specific target market.)

Trivia Carpets by Trivers

Look at Trivia Carpets by Trivers (Figure 10-2). In this case, A would be "new homes," A1 would be "tract builder," and A2 would indicate "custom builders."

The tract-builder target market is twice the size of the custom-builders target market, but the gross profit is very low. Should Trivers continue to market to both target markets? Could he make more money becoming a specialist for just one of these types of builders? The numbers don't contain the answers, but Trivers knows the questions to ask to find the answers and he can begin to make an informed decision rather than shoot from the hip. Good-bye, marketing gunslinger. Hello, smart marketer.

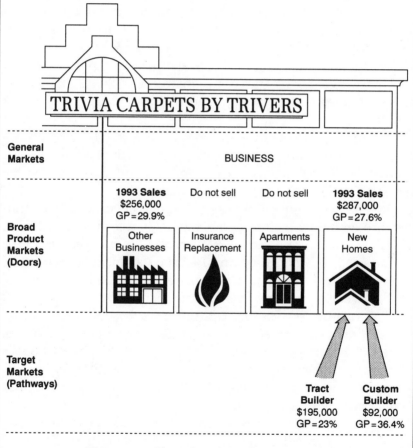

Figure 10-2. The value of the target markets.

Conclusion

The segmenting of business markets is a process of refining (reducing) the business markets into usable components. You will know the sales and profitability of the broad product markets (doors), of the target markets (pathways), and of the individual businesses.

Most retailers believe they already know this information—it's in their head. Intuitively, they have a sense of where their business comes from. But it has been my experience that store owners do not *really* know where their sales and profits come from. When I ask a floor-covering specialty store owner, "What percentage of your business is new-home construction?" I am told, "It's about 25%, wouldn't you say, Jack?" Jack the partner replies, "No, it's more like 45% or 50%." The correct answer is neither! Asking what gross profit their new-home construction business generates would be futile.

It is not good enough—ever—to "kinda know" where sales and profits are coming from. The smart Main Street retailer knows exactly who their core customer is and how much dollar volume and profit dollars the core customer delivers.

Remember, business success or failure is never equally distributed throughout your store. Sadly, the 20/80 rule applies to failure as well as to success. When a retailer, *who has not segmented their markets,* says, "Business is down 10%," the statement is of no value. The entire store does not have a decrease of 10% in all departments, but the owner only knows the one number—10%.

The retailer *who has segmented their markets will know exactly where and what the problem is:* "Our largest target market (core) is down 35% because our biggest single customer (Jones Builder) is testing a new marketing program with our competitor. We are off 47% with Jones Builder. The rest of our business is strong, but we're down 10% for the store."

The sales decreases exist for both retailers described here, but the retailer who has segmented their markets has the information to act. The other retailer will just keep wondering and looking.

SEGMENTING STEPS—CONSUMER MARKET

Segmenting the consumer market involves a different process than the one used for the business market. The identification of broad product markets (doors) and determining the volume/ profitability is completed the same way as for the business market. However, when you try to find your target markets (pathways), you won't break down the components, but rather add up individual customers in an attempt to find similarities. I'll show you how.

Step 1
Identify broad product markets (doors) in which you are presently selling. Determine volume and profitability.

This is completed the same way as the business market. The first step is to divide the consumer market into broad product markets (doors). You should assign short names to each door, and all employees should clearly understand the different broad product markets you serve.

How to Compute the Numbers

For planning and goal-setting purposes, each broad product market should be budgeted on a quarterly basis for sales and gross profit. If you're a big-ticket retailer (one who sells more expensive, larger items, like carpet or furniture), code the sales checks. Make it compatible with the code you used for broad product markets for the business section. If you're a small-ticket retailer (one who regularly sells less-expensive items like yogurt or small gifts), use your register or computer to code your consumer broad product markets. Employees must know that when they ring up a sale, they also will hit a special key to identify the correct broad product market. (If you have many *items* and are using a sku identifier number for inventory control, you will need to add a letter to identify the broad product market—for example, A92345, where A signifies the correct broad product market and the numbers identify the item as a stock number for reorder.)

Trivia Carpets by Trivers

Trivia Carpets by Trivers is a big-ticket retailer, but also regularly sells small items. He has given his consumer doors special names and the salespeople know how to code their sales checks and, for the smaller items, how to input the correct code in the computer.

Now, Trivers has complete information on the size and profitability of his broad product market segments on both sides of the store (Figure 10-3).

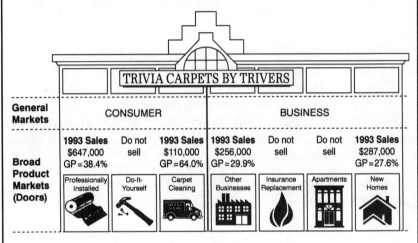

Figure 10-3. The store as separate markets.

Step 2
Determine the group of key demographic characteristics that impact the customers' buying decision for each broad product market (doors). These marketing descriptors will be used to find the target markets (pathways).

This is the most vexing part of segmenting and understanding customers. You want to know your customers as real people, not just as an income or age bracket. Manufacturers spend millions on this very issue of describing their core customers in the most complete and useful marketing terms. You can tell from national TV advertising that many manufacturers still haven't figured this out.

But that is not a reason to avoid this essential marketing task. The Main Street retailer must know the customer better than the competition does.

What is important about your core customer as it relates to your store and your different broad product markets? As I mentioned in Chapter 9, Markets, there are four demographic factors that must be part of your customer description: sex, age, income, and place of residence. In most cases, you need to add at least two more factors that affect the buying decision. You will know what other factors are important by listening to your customer.

Trivia Carpets by Trivers

Trivers listened to his customers, sought advice from his suppliers and trade associations, talked to his employees, added some common sense to the equation, and found the key demographic factors for his three broad product markets in the consumer section. Figure 10-4 shows what he discovered.

Let's examine the "professionally installed" market (door). Anybody who owns a home is a potential customer for the professionally installed market. Renters are not. (Trivers knows from his customers this is not the case for "carpet cleaning" or the "do-it-yourself" markets, a certain percentage of which are renters. Generally, renters have damaged or ruined the carpet, and want cheap, new carpet or pretty intense cleaning, but renters do represent part of the potential market.)

Children at home or no children are two important demographic factors. Trivers knows that customers without children are less concerned with durability and stain resistance and more interested in a wide color selection. Families with children feel obligated to be practical (wearability, hiding dirt, and stain resistance) first, and consider design and color second.

Marital status is also important. Married couples share the purchase decision. A single person with no children has different concerns than a single head of household with children.

Sex is probably the least important demographic factor. (I know I said it is relevant to all retail purchases regardless of product, but it is not as important as other factors.) Age, income, and location of home (the other basic demographic factors all retailers should know about their customers) are very important influences for customers buying installed carpet.

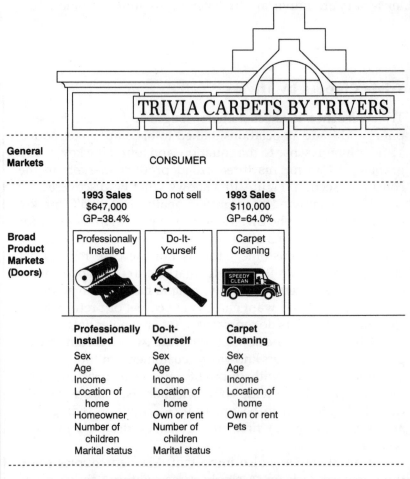

Figure 10-4. Describing customers.

Step 3
Find out where they live, how much they make, and what sex they are.

Step 3 takes time. You will build up this customer profile one customer at a time. It will take some discipline on your employees' part, but soon it will be a regular part of their job. You will notice patterns and they will help define the core customer and other target markets.

Many consultants tell retailers they get their largest percentage of volume from consumers who live closest to their store and less volume from consumers who live farther away from the store. This is called the theory of concentric circles. Take a look at Figure 10-5.

Do you think your sales volume fits into this concentric pattern? If you do, it's because you haven't completed the task of finding out where your customers live. There are always natural and man-made barriers to where customers go. If a store is close to a freeway, it is more apt to draw from farther away. If customers have to cross a bridge or use a two-lane, winding road (even though the store is close by), they well might not visit your store. One-way streets can make a store easy or more difficult to reach.

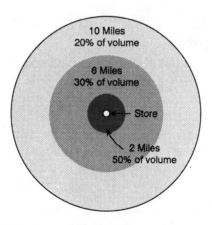

Figure 10-5. Customer location: theory of concentric circles.

The concentric-circle idea does not work for the Main Street retailer. There are many man-made barriers in your town, and people who have similar demographic characteristics, tastes, and lifestyles tend to congregate together. They also respond to similar marketing efforts and buy similar products.

Birds of a feather cluster together. It's simple, and true.

How to Map Out Your Customers and Determine Their Income

To complete Step 3, buy a large map of your marketing area. Place a pin on the map for each customer's home address. I have worked the pin method for more than 20 retailers. When completed, none of the 20 marketing maps reflected the concentric-circle idea. All of them reflected the kind of clustering I call "birds of a feather cluster together." Figure 10-6 illustrates this pattern.

For big-ticket retailers like Trivia Carpets by Trivers, place a pin on the map for each customer's home address. (Use a white

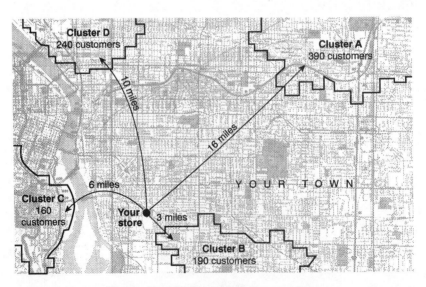

Figure 10-6. Where your customers live.

pin for female, red for male, and if marital status is important, green for married.) If they make a second purchase within six months, place another pin next to the first one. Those clients (repeat buyers) are your potential advocates.

You will not see clusters in the form of concentric circles; the pattern will reflect the birds of a feather phenomenon. Where you have clusters, draw a circle around the addresses, but give ample room beyond the addresses that are farthest away but, by your guess, are still part of the cluster. You should end up with two or three distinct pin-cluster areas. You also will find that 20% to 30% of the addresses that do not fit in any of the clusters.

Ask a local realtor friend to examine your map. Your friend can provide average home value for your cluster areas. (One of your market cluster areas may contain two different home value ranges. Use both, don't average.) Divide the home value by three. Presto, you have created a fairly accurate income range for your customer. Do that for each market cluster.

If one of your market clusters is predominantly apartments, multiply the average monthly rent by four and you now have a range for monthly income. Multiply by 12 for annual salary.

Do this for six months. Repeat for the same time period every year, on a different map. You will now know three demographic factors that are important for your retail marketing: the sex, income, and location of your customers.

It is extremely difficult to use a sales ticket with a name and address for every purchase from a small-ticket retailer, such as a gift store. (Radio Shack does this for all purchases, regardless of size, but it is very annoying to go through the Radio Shack drill for a $.99 battery. I don't recommend this approach.) For a designated period of time (three months for a small-ticket retailer), ask every customer for their ZIP code and telephone prefix. Enter the information into your computer or check it off on a spreadsheet by the register. Use a different spreadsheet for male and female. Once a week place pins in the different ZIP/prefix area. (When you buy your map for your marketing area, take it to the post office and then the phone company, and they will show you the areas covered for their respective identifiers. Generally the ZIP code represents a larger area, the phone prefix a smaller one.) Do this for three fairly busy months, and repeat the following year, in the same months, using a different map.

This map will not be as precise as the one for big-ticket retailers, but it will create identifiable clusters that become your core and secondary geographic areas.

The pin-cluster market profile is the best form of Main Street market research I know. It uses your customers to tell you their demographics themselves. You control the research, it's free, and it gives you much useful information.

Trivia Carpets by Trivers

It was a different story at Trivia Carpets by Trivers. Trivers hated the pin-cluster idea. It was "Mickey Mouse and too time consuming." However, he eventually relented and completed his big-ticket analysis, customer by specific customer. (Based on this pin-cluster work and some follow-up research, he devised a targeted advertising and promotion plan that was less expensive than his previous advertising approach, which was to "throw it against the wall, and then throw some more." I will cover his targeted advertising plan in Chapter 11, Building Markets and Creating Benefits.) Figure 10-7 shows Trivers's marketing area and the information he has now collected.

Trivers can describe, with absolute assurance, his core customers by sex, marital status, income, and location of their home:

Married
Income $45,000–$65,000
Live in either cluster A or B

He has now begun to build a real, comprehensive profile of his core customers, and his best guess is that there are 8,700 more married homeowners at the $45,000–$65,000 income level who live in clusters A and B and have not bought from him. Long before he starts looking at cluster C, he will direct his marketing dollars at clusters A and B. Because this research cost nothing and was not delivered in a leather-bound brochure, it should not be undervalued. Trivers is justifiably proud of this street-smart research.

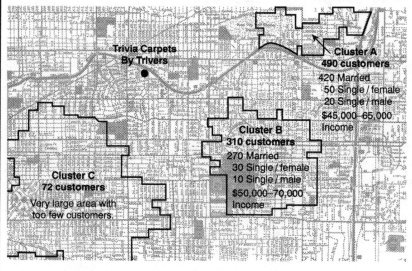

Figure 10-7. Location, sex, and income of customers.

Step 4
Research customers' age and additional demographic factors important to their buying habits.

Step 4 takes consumer research. You can't infer this information, or guess; you must ask the customer directly. It's simple. At the same time you are building your pin-cluster profile map, ask your customers questions that you cannot guess or infer from other data. The key is to ask the same customers you used for your pin research. They'll usually be happy to help in this customer research program. They will see it as an opportunity to help your business become more useful to them. By structuring the questionnaire correctly, you will gain important demographic information, customer critiques of your business, and customer loyalty, all at the same time: it's a 3-for-1 sale that costs pennies and helps create advocates for your store!

How to Complete the Research

Devise a simple questionnaire to gain the demographic information you want. Even though you already know the results from your pin work, include a question about income and sex. It will help validate your pin-cluster profile and assure the accuracy of the complete profile of your core customers and smaller target markets. Also, include five or six questions about your store operation and leave an area for customers to write anything they want. (Do not minimize the power of questions like: "What do you think?" and "How am I doing?") This entire questionnaire is an exercise in listening naively.

For a big-ticket retailer, mail the questionnaire with your thank-you card. For a small-ticket retailer, place the questionnaire in the bag, and ask that it be returned as soon as possible.

Some guidelines for the questionnaire:

1. Print no more than 10 questions on one side of the paper and leave an area for customers to write anything they want.
2. Ask customers if they would like to fill out the questionnaire while they're in the store. If not, they can mail it in, but you must include a self-addressed, stamped envelope. That stamp will improve your response rate dramatically.
3. The questionnaire should look professional.
4. Start with a simple explanation of what you're trying to do. "In a continuing effort to improve our service, and better understand our customer. . . ."
5. If appropriate, use a range rather than the specific number. Age: 35–44, 45–54; income: $30,000–$40,000.
6. The questions about store operation can be very specific, "Has our new voice-mail system improved our service?" or, more

general, "Please rate our promptness in solving complaints." Regardless, always include, "What's the one thing you would change in our store?"

7. Assure anonymity. Customers are more apt to tell you what they think if they can remain faceless.

8. By combining demographic questions with questions about how they feel about your store, you will improve the response rate and receive helpful direction for improvement.

9. If you get over 30% response, you're doing great. They obviously like your store and weren't threatened by the questionnaire.

10. You will get your questionnaires back within two weeks of when customers receive it, or never, so you don't have to wait long to compile the total responses.

Trivia Carpets by Trivers

How did Trivers do with his consumer-research project? From the "What don't you like about our store," question, Trivers was surprised (that's an understatement) to learn about his customers' disappointment with his new voice-mail system which was fairly expensive. Many customers disliked punching numbers instead of talking to a human. They didn't think voice mail improved service at Trivia Carpets by Trivers. Whoever sold him the voice-mail system hopefully has a generous return policy because they're about to get one back, barely used.

With the new demographic information, Trivers looked for meaningful clusters to add to his pin-cluster profile, which included income, sex, marital status, and home location information. Trivers felt that, in addition to age, the number of children in the household influenced the purchasing decision and, therefore, was important to his total customer profile. Figure 10-8 shows what information Trivers compiled on his customers' age and number of children living at home.

Trivers was looking to see if the age and number of children of his customers clustered together (like the geographic cluster). They did. You can see how he created two meaningful clusters: age 36–45, one or more children; and the other distinct group, age 51 and above, with no children. The cluster group, younger with children, would be part of his core customer definition.

| | Children at home | | |
	No children	One child	Two or more children
25–30	—	—	—
31–35	—	—	16
36–40	—	46	246
41–45	6	136	184
46–50	11	20	73
51–55	71	5	6
56+	42	—	—

(Row label axis: **Age**)

Figure 10-8. Number of children at home.

Step 5
Combine pin-cluster information with consumer research. Describe core customer and other important target markets (pathways).

Combine the clusters. Take the pin-cluster information and overlay the additional demographic information from your consumer research. You should see one or two core markets and no more than two other, smaller target markets (pathways) for each broad product market (door) in the consumer section of your store. This is the final step in segmenting your customers.

Unlike the business market, you will not know the exact volume the core customer delivers. You will know what percentage of customers are core, but you won't know exactly how much they buy. Again, it would be very rare if a core customer or any customer group did not have sales equal to their number as individual customers.

Trivia Carpets by Trivers

When Trivers combined the pin-cluster information and consumer research, he found his core customer for professionally installed carpet:

> Married
> Income $45,000–$65,000
> Lives in two areas he has marked as clusters A and B
> Age 36–45
> One or more children at home

He also discovered a secondary target market for professionally installed carpet:

> Married
> Income $45,000–$65,000
> Lives in areas he has marked as clusters A and B
> Age 51+
> No children at home

This method of finding and defining your customer is imperfect. Trivers does not know if there are more older customers in cluster A or B, but by asking about income and sex he can prevent a statistical anomaly, such as whether a larger percentage of the 51+ group earns near the top of the income bracket. Regardless, he has information that he can promote and advertise against. He now knows where his customers live and who the core customer is, and he has a very good idea about the smaller target market.

Conclusion

Without a doubt, the task of segmenting the consumer market is the most difficult marketing task you will face. It is hard work, but the reward is that you will know your customers better than your competition does, and that's the battle you want to win.

Remember, marketing is intensely analytical, and segmenting your consumer market is the most intense part.

Most Main Street retailers I know skip segmenting and go right to advertising and promoting their business. Retail is, after all, action and most retailers like to get right to the action of advertising. But traditional advertising is a very sloppy and wasteful form of communication and if you don't complete the job of segmenting, it's even more expensive and wasteful.

I believe that 90% to 95% of those who see your advertisement or commercial have no interest in the product at that time and they glaze over the message, which is wasted on those people. It's the same when you buy a new car. Before you purchased your new Lexus or whatever, you only knew two people who owned one like it, and you only saw a few around town. After you purchased your car, you recognize it everywhere. You're surprised there are so many cars like yours. Before you paid no attention, now you do. Unless you're actively in the market for the product, you don't see the ad.

That's why segmenting is such an important part of the process of finding customers. In its most basic form, segmenting reduces the waste in communication. Only 50% won't care about your product, but, that's quite an improvement over the "Let's get this ad run and get some traffic in the store" approach. In that example, 95% won't see your ad.

You will learn in the next chapter, Building Markets and Creating Benefits, how to listen to your core and secondary customers, and devise a plan to attract more like them.

GETTING DOWN TO BUSINESS

Applying Marketing Principles to Your Business

SEGMENTING

Segmenting is the process of sorting, organizing, and describing broad product and target markets.

No questions this time.

I've prepared a checklist of segmenting steps you should use every year. Make them part of your store's marketing habits.

Segmenting Business Markets

1. Describe all broad product markets (doors) in which you could participate.
2. Code all sales checks. Every purchase must be assigned a specific broad product market (door).
3. Total on a monthly basis and evaluate quarterly. After the first year, set up a spreadsheet with budgeted goals and actual results.
4. Complete steps 2 and 3 for each target market (pathway) and individual business customer.

Segmenting Consumer Markets

1. Describe all broad markets (doors) in which you could participate.
2. Decide what is most important about your customers and the products they buy that affect their buying decision. Include sex, age, income, and place of residence and add other factors as required.
3. For a specific period of time, utilize the pin-cluster method and consumer research to identify core customers and smaller target customers (pathways).
4. Combine or overlay the above information. Describe core customer and any smaller customer groups (pathways).

11

BUILDING MARKETS AND CREATING BENEFITS

DEFINITION
Building markets and creating benefits involves building sales by finding more customers like the ones you have, seeking new target markets (pathways), and creating new business opportunities (doors).

After you have segmented your markets, there are three ways to find new customers and build your sales:

1. *"New like old."* Find new customers who behave and look like your existing core and secondary customers.
2. *"New pathway."* Promote and advertise to a customer group that has shown little or no interest in your store.
3. *"New door."* Create a new business opportunity by developing a broad product market (door) that you had previously disregarded.

The process for business and consumer markets is similar, but the method of communication is different. Since there are so few customers involved in the business market, all communication with prospective business customers should be on a one-to-one basis— direct and personal. The method of communication is more complex for the consumer market, but it's important to be *direct* in this market also.

For both markets (business and consumer), you first must listen naively to your core customers, offer the prospective customers those benefits they want (act direct), and do so in a more compelling way than your competition.

BUSINESS MARKET

New Like Old

This is always the first and best place to start when looking for new customers. *It's easier, smarter, and cheaper to find new customers who behave like your existing customers.* They are seeking the same benefits, so you don't have to add three new services to your business to gain their acceptance.

If New Like Old is best, New Like Core is the best of the best. Start with your core business customers of your most successful broad product market (door).

Listen Naively

Tell your core customers you want to listen and learn about their business. (I know you talk with these people every day, but this must be different. This must occur in a more formal setting, face to face; take notes and do very little talking.)

Invite 10 of your best business customers to this round table. Be sure to leave the meeting with a clear understanding of what the customers think you do right. It is also very important for you to know about their customers' concerns. (If you know your customers and the benefits they seek, that's good; if you know your customers' customers and the benefits your customers' customers seek, that's great! You will always be able to make a powerful marketing presentation to a prospective business customer. Your customers will be very impressed.)

Ask your business customers for a letter of recommendation and the names of five to seven businesses who the core customers will call on your behalf. Don't be shy. Remember, a happy customer loves to tell friends!

Even though you are seeking help from happy core customers to find new customers (you are asking your customers to become advocates), you also are keeping in touch to be sure there isn't something you should change or do to keep the core customers happy. Always ask how your company can be more convenient to them. Remember, running out of time and never catching up is the enemy of their business. If you become more convenient to them, their advocacy is assured.

Next, talk and listen naively to your employees. Any employee who has any contact (shipping, billing, etc.) with the core customers should be part of the discussion. Share with them what the core customers told you. Brainstorm. Every idea is worthy. It's possible your employees are doing things that the core customer thinks is very helpful and you don't know anything about it. (When you make presentations to prospective businesses, you should include these benefits.)

Last, do a little skulking around the prospective businesses you want to sell. Visit their business and ask questions about the operation. Get any information about them that can help you address specific concerns they might have that are different from your core customers'.

Now you're ready to make the sales pitch.

Act Direct

Your core customer has made contact with a similar business to theirs and has recommended you. You have made an appointment to visit the owner. Prepare a proposal, specific to this business, with at least three letters of endorsement. That's why I call this "Act Direct." Everything in the package is directed at this company, the way it operates, and the benefits that you know it is seeking. (This is another reason why you should have a computer. The proposal, with the customer's name emblazoned on the cover, should look professional. Don't underestimate the value of a personalized, professionally organized, but very inexpensive presentation package. People love to see their name.)

Suggestions for your Act Direct promotional package:

1. Put the customer's name, name of company, and date on the front cover.

2. Put the specific proposal first, followed by support material.
3. Give a short history of your company; list awards and membership in professional organizations. List nonprofit organizations you support.
4. Include why your company sells to this specific type of business. Explain the benefits your core customers receive from your company. (Include benefits your employees told you about.)
5. Demonstrate your knowledge of your core customer's *customer*.
6. Explain how you have helped your core customer become more profitable.
7. Rate yourself for convenience quotient.
8. Tell the customer why you would like them to be part of your core customer group. Tell them how you listened to your core customer, your employees, and their employees for this presentation. (They will love your resourcefulness; you know it's just smart marketing.)
9. Explain how and why there is a "marketing fit" between the two companies.
10. Always keep a copy of the presentation folder. If they don't want to join your core club, you'll know exactly what you told them. They'll be back, or you will.

The one thing you should not do, under any circumstances, is blindly send out a brochure to 50 or 500 prospective businesses. You might know everything about what you want to sell, but you know nothing of the benefits the customer might be seeking. Brochures try to stay in the middle and satisfy a generalized population of prospective customers. Using such brochures, you don't take the ultimate risk in marketing: "Be something special to a specific customer, otherwise you will be nothing to everyone." I don't care how pretty the brochure is, its life on the receiving end is milliseconds.

When marketing to other businesses, you will find a big difference between mass-mailing a brochure to a fairly specific group of businesses, and the smart, Act Direct marketing approach. It's the difference between success and failure.

Trivia Carpets by Trivers

Trivers knows the difference. When Trivia Carpets was an "un-marketing" company, it sent out 57 brochures to new-home builders in its marketing area. Only two responded; neither decided to use Trivia Carpets' program.

With his newfound marketing insight, Trivers reevaluated the new-home market (door). Figure 11-1 shows how it segmented.

As I stated in Chapter 9, Markets, Trivers saw a problem with the compatibility of the benefits the tract builder sought versus the benefits the custom builder needed. Profitability was an issue. The tract builder was twice the size in volume ($195,000 vs. $92,000 for custom builders) but generated a very low gross profit (23% vs. 36.4% for custom builders). Trivers wasn't overpaying for the carpet the tract builders used; the tract builders wanted minimum standard carpet and always looked for the lowest price to protect the lowest possible cost for the entire new home.

The more Trivers looked at the custom-builder market, the more he realized these builders fit well with his company, whereas the tract market was a marginal fit. Trivers felt that his store delivered the benefits the custom builders sought (excellent, personalized service) and he could generate the same profit dollars on far less volume. He decided to build this target market. Custom builders would be his core market for the new-homes broad product market (door).

Trivers followed the New Like Old plan. He listened naively to the largest and most loyal custom builders. He did the same with his employees. (His core customers credited him for something he felt sure his people weren't doing. He rushed back to tell them to implement this new way of identifying the carpet. They all chuckled; the receiving manager had made that change four months earlier. The sidemarking of carpet became an important benefit that Trivers offered his prospective customers.) He did some skulking, and the smartest listening naively occurred when he visited two customers (homeowners) of each custom builder to whom he wanted to sell.

When Trivers made his "Act Direct" presentation, he

knew his prospective customers (custom-home builders) and he knew their customers (homeowners). He had a satisfied customer (home builder) endorse his store and delivered a professional presentation tailored to each prospective custom builder. Most were very impressed.

Trivia Carpets will begin to decrease sales to tract builders. Even though the total carpet sales to the custom-builder market is about one-third of potential carpet sales to the tract-builder market, Trivers has decided to become the best carpet supplier for the custom builders in his trading area. That's narrowcasting, and his existing, happy customers (advocates) are going to help him build that market.

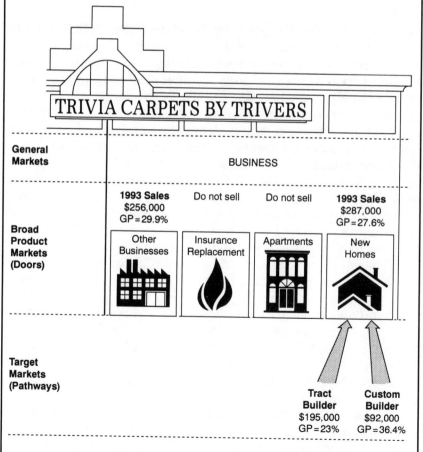

Figure 11-1. Analysis of true value of target markets.

New Pathway

It's easy to find a different target market (pathway) that is only occasionally buying from you but represents a large segment of potential customers. Since you have segmented your markets, you know they exist. Every three months you review the sales and profits of your broad product markets (doors), your target markets (pathways), and your specific business customers. Once a year you should evaluate those target markets that are represented by only a few companies who rarely buy from you. These are indifferent customers, not clients. Consequently, you have treated them with benign neglect. That's fine, they weren't important to you. But should they be?

Listen Naively

You must answer the question, "Are they (the potential target market) a large market and are they compatible with my core customer?" Your banker, local Small Business Development Center, Chamber of Commerce, or industry association and journals should be able to help you determine the size of this target market. If the answer is Yes to the question of size, you must consider their compatibility with your core customer. Size and growth of a potential new target market (pathway) are not reason enough to pursue this target market. They must also be compatible.

Compatibility relates to the benefits both customer groups seek. If this potential new target market wants totally different benefits than you are offering your core customers, you will risk confusing or offending your core customers and worse, they will begin to think you are not committed to them.

The only way to answer the compatibility question is to listen naively to these prospective customers. You must sit down with the few customers (from this potential key target market) who buy from you and at least 10 who don't and let them talk about their business. A key question you want answered is, "Why aren't you buying from me?" The answer invariably will be one of two things: Either you don't offer the benefits they need to be successful, or an image the competition created for you makes you look less than desirable.

Ultimately, you must return to the issue of compatibility. If this target market is very large and your mouth waters at the possibilities of greatness, but they need a whole new set of benefits than the ones you're offering, you must pass. Take their money when they come to your store, but don't market to them. It is better to be something special to a specific target market, otherwise you will be nothing to everyone, and no one will be happy with you.

On the other hand, if this target market's needs are compatible with the benefits you now offer, you need to begin convincing the target market that you are the best supplier for their needs. I don't care how bad the competition has portrayed you, if the benefits this target market wants are compatible with those benefits your core customers know you are delivering, then it's time to get aggressive with this new target market. Challenging the competition is a lot easier than changing the benefits you offer. The first requires marketing skills, the second will lead to your business obituary.

If the benefits match up (core customer and potential new target market), kick into high gear:

1. Visit with the business owners of all those who participated in your listen naively sessions.
2. Ask about their business. They will be impressed that you are taking the time to learn more about them.
3. Visit with their customer's customer.
4. Have one or two key employees do some skulking at the same businesses.
5. Talk and listen naively to your employees.

You're ready to make your sales pitch.

Act Direct

Start with a simple Act Direct promotional package (see pages 174–175). The key is to create a personalized, professionally organized, and inexpensive package.

You won't have third-party endorsements from satisfied customers in this target market. Unlike your core target market, you won't have the help of your core customers advocating your business. So, you'll have to start with those few businesses who have bought from you occasionally. They have some personal knowledge of your store and should be easier to convince than a business that has never come to your store and only knows you through rumor and kind words from your competitors.

Be persistent. You have listened naively to them, created a professional brochure based on their suggestions (the brochure is a powerful visual of your commitment to their target market), and taken the time to visit their store and learn about their operation. Business owners are like anyone else: They love to be wanted. You have demonstrated your commitment to their business. You'll sign up some of your occasional customers as the new core customers for this target market (pathway).

After you have signed up a few customers, stop selling. Spend three months refining your operation and fixing any unplanned problems. Then take the same approach to the next group who participated in your listen naively session. Sign some up. Stop selling. Fix problems. Continue the cycle.

Trivia Carpets by Trivers

When Trivers made his annual review of target markets (pathways) that he had treated with benign neglect, he decided to look at the pathways that led to the broad product market (door) he had labeled "Other Businesses" (see Figure 11-2).

Trivers visited the local Small Business Development Center, which had industry sales listed by business segment. He realized he was just skimming the "Other Businesses" market. This broad product market (door) represented 30% of all carpet sales, but it only represented 14% of Trivia Carpets' volume. He was selling to banks and other multichain businesses. When he made his Act Direct presentation to these companies, he made the sale. But the small independent retailers and service companies (a target market or pathway) rarely bought carpet from Trivia Carpets. Trivers was unavailable for these customers on a day-to-day basis and the floor salespeople didn't really have the expertise to sell to this target market. And Trivers's competitors told the independent, single-store retailers and service companies that Trivers only liked the "big boys."

Small businesses represented a very large segment of the carpet sales in Trivers's marketing area. When he talked to the few small-business customers who bought from him, he realized they sought the same benefits he was offering the large banks. He just didn't have a full-time person committed to this target market (pathway). The small businesses wanted to deal with a specialist. So Trivers hired a "business carpet" specialist. For him, Marketing Principle 2 makes complete sense: "The outside (customer) determines what the inside (organization) looks like and how it operates." Now, when the competition bad-mouths Trivia Carpets by Trivers for being out of touch with independent retailers and the benefits they seek, he has a person and plan to change that image.

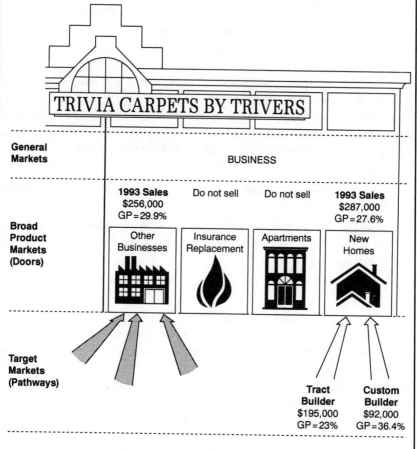

Figure 11-2. Expanding the pathway.

New Door

Peter Drucker, the well-known management consultant and professor of social sciences at the Claremont Graduate School in southern California, has chastised big businesses for "feeding problems and starving opportunities." He suggests Sears has been doing just that. For the Main Street retailer, damage control or problem solving is an everyday occurrence; in fact, it can consume all your time. But if you truly want to expand existing markets (New Like Old program) or build new broad product markets (doors), you have to pull back from the everyday unplanned chaos. Otherwise, you'll never see or appreciate the opportunities. Problem solving is rearguard action; you stop the hemorrhaging, but that's about it.

The right opportunities create growth. Looking at broad product markets (doors) you are not *serving is another smart way to feed opportunities and build markets.*

Are there broad product markets (doors) you are not serving? Each year you should consider why you are not serving these markets. Do not accept the excuses, "We haven't done it before," or "I don't understand it, it will be too much hassle." Give real thought to the market opportunity. Ask three questions:

1. Will our core customers benefit from this new business opportunity?
2. Will another customer group, who is compatible with my core customer but has not bought from me, benefit from this new business opportunity?
3. Can I make a profit from this investment within one year?

Obviously, this book cannot assist in the financial analysis which must be completed to ensure the idea is financially viable, but I can suggest ideas to help ensure customers will be receptive to a new business opportunity and to determine whether that opportunity might conflict with your present customers or enhance your relationship with them.

If you answer Yes to Questions 1 and 2, you should proceed to a full financial analysis of the idea.

How do you get answers to Questions 1 and 2?

Listen Naively

Find a retailer outside your trading area who is serving the broad product market (door) you are considering. You should have a network of four or five retailers who will share with you all aspects of their business. It's called "trustworthy" market research. It's much better to go outside your trading area to complete your trustworthy market research because any business you talk to is not a potential customer—it will be more objective and you'll get the straight scoop. Later, when you visit businesses you might want to sell in your marketing area, you won't go in there as a complete novice. You'll be better equipped to evaluate what they say and what they mean.

Visit your friends and review, in depth, how they have set up their marketing program to serve this broad product market (door). Also, talk to at least 10 of your friends' customers. What you want to find out from the retailer's customers is:

1. Are they like your core customers?
2. If not, would they be compatible with your core customers?
3. Are the benefits they seek from this broad product market (door) similar to those your store offers?
4. Do they know businesses in your trading area that are using this service? Ask them to profile (size, how they run their business, integrity, etc.) these potential customers.

After you have completed the initial trustworthy market research, determine the fit. Are your friends' customers like your core customer and do they seek the same benefits from this broad product market (door) that you are presently delivering for other products and services? If the answer is Yes, set up as many meetings as you need to talk to 25 of *your* core business customers. Explain to them your business opportunity. You need to determine three facts from your core customers:

1. Are they presently buying this program or service from someone else?

2. If so, what does the competition do right? What does it do wrong?
3. Do they know users of this program or service who are not customers of your store? Get names.

This is still market research. You want to determine your present core business customer's satisfaction with their existing supplier, if the benefits they seek are compatible with your store's strengths, and what it will take to get their business.

You have listened naively. Thanks to your friend, you now know how to operate this new broad product market (door). You have listened naively to two sets of customers: your friend's and your own core customers. You know exactly what benefits the customer expects from this new venture and the weaknesses of your competition. If the financial analysis says, "Go," I say, "Go!"

Act Direct

Treat the opening of a new broad product market (door) the same way you would announce the opening of a new store—with lots of fanfare and excitement, all with the understanding that you have a new and better way of serving this major market. You may actually use a brochure and run an ad. Here are my suggestions:

1. Run a small newspaper campaign announcing the Grand Opening of this new marketing program.
2. Send a press release to all media. Try to get the newspaper to run an article at the same time as your advertising campaign for this program.
3. Run an ad in your Chamber of Commerce newsletter announcing the new program.
4. The first three suggestions are not really Act Direct–type advertising. That's okay. You want the community to know you're doing something big. People will see your Main Street retail store as a progressive, action-oriented business. That will help all facets of your business.

5. Send an inexpensive three-fold, two-color brochure (8½″ × 11″ paper folded to make three panels) announcing your new program to all your present business customers. Invite them to an open house for your new broad product market (door). Offer some gift or incentive for the owner to bring another business owner to the event.

6. Do not sign up any businesses at the open house. This is just to get leads.

7. Make appointments. Use the Act Direct promotional package, with the customer's name on the front of the book and a personalized presentation. It is so much better to do it this way than signing up many business customers only to find they expected one thing and you delivered another. Take your time. Business relationships based on complete understanding will always last longer than the expedient, "Let's sell it today, we'll sweat the small stuff tomorrow."

With a new business opportunity, always go to your other core business customers to start up the new venture. Don't assume that everything will be fine because they know you. Take the time to present your program to them, personalize it, and you will have created an advocate for many years to come.

Trivia Carpets by Trivers

One last look at the business market (Figure 11-3) of Trivia Carpets by Trivers.

Trivers had not actively marketed to the apartment broad product market (door). Recent reports in *Floor Covering News* (one of the carpet industry's magazines) indicated a substantial growth in carpet sales to apartment owners and developers. Trivers had stayed away from this business. He decided to make a complete review of this potential new market for his Main Street retail store.

To complete some trustworthy market research, Trivers visited a friend (another retailer) who introduced him to seven

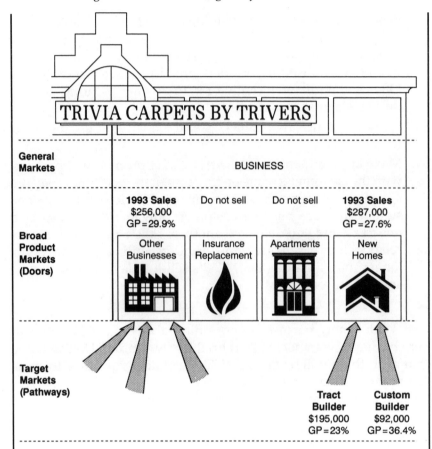

Figure 11-3. Viewing business opportunities.

apartment managers and developers. They seemed to seek benefits that Trivers was not presently offering his other business customers: inexpensive carpet, narrow assortment, and instant installation. His friend's operation confirmed the apartment customers' views. It was like tract homes, but cheaper. Cheap carpet installed the day after move-out, which is the day before move-in by a new tenant.

None of Trivers's core customers was an apartment owner or developer, so armed with this market information (the benefits the apartment owners sought) he visited five local apartment owners. They told him they would like a wide assortment and personalized service, and that price and fast installation were important, but not as important as assortment and personalized service. This made no sense to Trivers. If they wanted the same benefits on which he had built his company's reputation, he surely would have had a few key customers from the apartment market, but he didn't. Trivers decided that his trustworthy market research was accurate, but the local apartment owners were telling him what he wanted to hear, not what actually was needed.

This business opportunity was not a good fit (compatible) with Trivers's existing operation. He decided not to pursue this business opportunity, but learned a valuable lesson: Many customers will tell you what they think you want to hear. You then jump in, become their supplier, and find out to your dismay that what they really expect from you is not what you're set up to deliver. That's why you should leave town to measure the customer's comments with the actual operation of your friends' stores. Only then will you be able to discuss with your local businesses the real issues. Get the harsh reality before you invest in a business opportunity that will not fit with your Main Street retail store.

Conclusion

Why can't you market to two broad product markets (doors) or target markets (pathways) that seek radically different benefits? You can, but it's not believable. Wal-Mart doesn't sell designer dresses and Nordstrom doesn't sell toilet paper at a low price. They have a position in the marketplace. That is their customers' image of their business and they will do everything to protect and enhance that image. That's the way they have built their markets.

They constantly look for new business opportunities (doors), new customers like their existing core customers, and new target markets (pathways) that are similar and compatible with their core customers. You should build markets and grow the same way.

CONSUMER MARKET

For the consumer market, you will still look at the three ways to build markets: New Like Old, New Pathways, and New Doors. Also, you will listen naively, but the method of communicating is not as direct nor as simple as with a prospective business customer. To build the consumer market successfully, you must know how to communicate with a large number of people in the most efficient and compelling way. That communication includes damnable, frustrating "If I only knew the right ad" advertising and promotions. Mass advertising and promotions are what distinguish building consumer markets from building business markets, and it is advertising and promotions that drive the Main Street retailers to despair. One ad brings in more customers than you can handle and the next ad is not read by two people in your entire marketing area. And nobody knows why.

I want to eliminate some of your frustration with advertising by giving you Mini Principles that should guide your approach to advertising and promotions.

ADVERTISING/PROMOTION PRINCIPLE 1
Build two signature promotions a year. Repeat every year.

It's better to create promotions than send out a mailer or advertising in the general media. Promotions are events, and advertising is one of the components. Promotions include any or all of these ideas: advertising, a display change in store, balloons, banners, employee outfits, employee incentives, customer contests, giveaways, other retailers participating, a tie-in with a local event, a tie-in with a nonprofit organization, and much more. The more the merrier.

Create two signature promotions a year and make them more powerful each year by increasing their number of elements. These two promotions will become your signature events. Over time, you want everyone, regardless of whether they need your product or not, to have top-of-the-mind awareness of your Main Street retail store name and these two promotions. You will create two White

Sales and everyone in town will know that only your store puts on this great, fun-filled event.

The reason you want to create two signature promotions is simple: dominance. Retail business may be competitive in your town, but the business of advertising and attempting to get a consumer to listen, watch, or read your message is brutally competitive. The United States represents 6% of the world's population, but consumes 57% of the world's advertising. Unless you live in a cave, you will receive about 200 commercial messages every day! Talk about information overload.

It is in this environment of confusing and contradictory promises hurled at the consumer that the Main Street retailer must find their voice—and hope someone is listening. A lot of small promotions and ads get lost in all the advertising clutter but your two signature promotions will ensure your message is seen and heard. For that short period you will have a dominant voice, not just because you out-advertised your competition, but because you created many different communication ideas to build a major event. By combining all the creative marketing elements for your two signature promotions, you achieve a synergy or power that exceeds the strength of each element taken separately. You also receive a residual benefit from these two promotions: Potential customers are more apt to pay attention to your other ads and promotions during the rest of the year.

Your marketing budget for finding customers should start with the two signature promotions (always repeated at the same time of year with the same theme). Fund those two promotions first. Do not plan any other advertising until you have planned and set aside the marketing dollars for the two promotions that will become your signature.

Each of these two signature promotions should meet some, if not all, of these criteria:

1. It should be a month-long event.
2. Timing is critical. It should run during the best sales period in the spring and the best sales period in the fall. Don't try to create an exciting event when customers are not naturally think-

ing about your product. "Christmas in July" is cute, but too counter-intuitive.

3. It must be timeless (White Sale), not just timely for this specific year ("Our roof caved in during the rains and we have soaked stuff"). You will repeat the same theme every year.

4. For the promotion period, your store must look different.

5. Give incentives to all your employees.

6. Try to find an angle for a press release. The more this becomes a community event (connected with a nonprofit organization), the more apt you are to get free publicity.

7. Your core customers should always be *the* target market you are talking to for these promotions.

Stephen Leacock, a very funny guy, defined advertising and promotion as the "science of arresting the human intelligence long enough to get money from it." When you build two signature promotions, you will "arrest" your core customers' attention and get lots of money from them and many who are like them. Like so many things, this marketing effort takes commitment, discipline, and planning. It will be justly rewarded.

ADVERTISING/PROMOTION PRINCIPLE 2
Promotions (even small ones) are better than
just advertising.

When possible, run promotions, don't just advertise. Advertising is one-dimensional; promotions are multidimensional. Creating distinctive promotions is always better than just running an ad. Promotions take more time and require some planning, but they're worth it. With promotions, you're more apt to get employee participation and have a more compelling idea than the typical, "We need some sales, let's reduce everything 30% and get some traffic." Unfortunately, that tactic is tried in too many Main Street retail stores—and it is never very successful.

Here are 10 ideas that you can convert into powerful promotions:

1. *Postcard promotion.* Send your prospective customers a blank postcard. Whoever can write your store name the most times on the postcard wins a prize. The card must be dropped off at the store.

2. *Private sale.* Hold a private sale, after regular store hours. Prospective customers must bring the official invitation to be admitted. Serve champagne. Have a drawing for a "private getaway."

3. *Halloween promotion.* Give away free pumpkins and hold a contest for the best-carved pumpkin. The pumpkin must be carved at the store and a picture taken of the finished pumpkin. The pumpkin can be taken home.

4. *Saturday-only balloon promotion.* Mail large imprinted balloons to prospective customers, who must come in to have them inflated. In the store, children can learn how to create balloon art (little balloons twisted into different shapes). Take pictures of the artist and art. If the big balloons get seen around town and some float away in your competitors' store, it's good for you!

5. *Radio personality.* Inform prospective customers by direct mail that a local radio personality will be at your store for three hours on the weekend or at night during the week. The personality will autograph T-shirts and hats. (You will pay more for this promotion, but the radio station will advertise the event on its own during the week prior.) This is an excellent use of direct mail and radio and should be part of the two signature promotions.

6. *Double-save promotion.* Reduce prices on a large assortment of products. The customer pays regular price but receives "funny money" which reflects the savings. Hold an auction with store merchandise every hour. Whoever is the highest bidder pays with funny money.

7. *"We gotta get rid of this stuff" Salvation Army sale.* This promotion must be approved by the Salvation Army or similar organization. List your old merchandise in alphabetical order, an item for every letter in the alphabet. Use fairly deep discounts. If prospective customers bring in an item with the same first letter as the product they want, you give them an additional

discount and donate the object they brought to the Salvation Army.

8. *Store birthday sale.* Everybody who will disclose their birthday can enter this contest. You are celebrating your store's birthday and send out a letter with a postcard enclosed. Prospective customers write their birthday on the postcard and send it in. That's all they do. You'll draw 10 names of persons who will be invited to celebrate your birthday with you at the store. You will get valuable information (birthdays) which you will put in your computer. From now on, you'll send a birthday card on their birthday.

9. *Our buddy sale.* Tie in with another retailer whose customers live in the same general area as yours. The mailing should not weigh more than a solo effort by yourself. This way you split the cost, but keep the distribution the same as if you were doing it yourself. Use the same signage in both stores.

10. *Trunk sales.* Any time you add a new supplier, new brand name from an existing supplier, or a new line of products, make a special announcement. It does not have to be a real trunk sale, but something like it is necessary. A special showing to special customers is always appreciated.

Don't underestimate the value of small promotions. They will cost a little more than running an ad, but watch the results. Your customers will respond to your creativity.

ADVERTISING/PROMOTION PRINCIPLE 3
The less you know about your customers, the more expensive it is to advertise and run promotions. The more you know about your customers, the less expensive it is to advertise and run promotions.

Do you dislike junk mail? I do. Most people dislike unsolicited catalogs and letters from businesses because they have no interest in the product or service. That mail is indeed junk and goes directly to the wastebasket. But if you are interested in the product or products offered (a friend who knows what you like tells Spiegel to mail you its most recent catalog), you keep the catalog, probably order something from it, and every subsequent catalog is happily received.

The difference between discarded junk mail and direct mail which is read is the difference between using mail as if it were TV (going to a large number of customers with no idea of who is interested in your product) and using mail as an individual medium to talk to those who are most apt to buy your product. You find those customers most apt to buy your product by segmenting your business. Direct mail then becomes the most efficient and least expensive medium.

Every program or section of each medium (newspaper, radio, TV, mail, even billboards) has a core customer (they are actually readers, viewers, or listeners). A certain well-described person is more likely to watch *Geraldo,* and I presume that a quite different person watches *MacNeil Lehrer News Hour.* But if you don't know your customer well enough, you won't know the best media or mix of media, much less the exact programs, to match to your customer. When you can't match your customers with the media's different audiences, you will try to communicate with a tremendous number of people, most of whom have no interest in your store or products. You will substitute quantity of readers, viewers, and listeners for the quality ones who are really interested in your product or service. Quantity is not the answer; you are producing "advertising pollution" or junk at a very high cost, and most people will ignore your message.

Regardless of the media you use, if you do not segment your consumer market and listen naively to your core customers, but advertise "because ya gotta advertise to get customers," you're wasting your money. That's not communicating. You will "arrest" few intelligent minds, and get even less money.

ADVERTISING/PROMOTION PRINCIPLE 4
Look at advertising and promotion as a marketing investment, not an expense. The investment is based on a fixed percentage of your future sales.

Don't look at advertising as an expense. Expenses can be deferred, delayed, reduced, or canceled. Much as you look at your monthly lease or mortgage payment for your Main Street retail store as an investment for a specific location and size of store, you should look at advertising and promotion as a specific way of communicating with your customers. Rather than a static monthly investment (like rent), you should spend your advertising and promotion money in direct relation to the sales you expect for a given period, usually a month.

Allocate your advertising and promotion dollars in relation to your sales volume, month by month. To do that, fix a percentage of your sales for the year's advertising and promotion. (I suggest that you ask your newspaper and TV stations for this information for your type of retail store. They have it for all stores in the United States like yours.) Use this percentage each month when you set your monthly sales budget. You have automatically set your advertising and promotion budget.

If your advertising is well timed and directed at your core customers and those like them, your monthly advertising/promotion pattern will mimic your monthly sales pattern. Figure 11-4 depicts the perfect pattern.

If your Main Street retail store achieved this perfect relationship between your advertising/promotion cost and sales results, you would be hailed as a combination Sam Walton and David Ogilvy (the modern advertising guru). Advertising/promotion precedes expected sales. You advertise/promote to build customer

Figure 11-4. A perfect sales and advertising curve.

awareness of an event or product and hope customers come to your store and buy as a result of your advertising/promotion. If you invested the right amount every time and met your sales goal every time so that your advertising cost was always the same percentage, you would have achieved marketing nirvana. Unfortunately, no company has ever achieved this marketing perfection. Most achieve the results seen in Figure 11-5.

Look at the two lines for May in Figure 11-5. This store spent a lot of money and sales were awful. In July, the opposite happened. There could be many reasons why the advertising delivered so few sales in May. I'm not suggesting you overanalyze this but, where there is little relationship between the advertising/promotion investment and expected sales, the store is typically approaching this marketing tactic as if advertising/promotion were an expense to be incurred only when the store needed sales or it was feeling particularly good about itself. Another way to look at this is, wherever sales and advertising/promotion lines don't correlate, you're missing selling opportunities with advertising that's run too early or too late.

Advertising/promotion, like any other marketing tactic, demands discipline. It is part science, part timing, part art, and part luck. If you discipline your investment to advertising/promotion with a fixed percentage set for the year and fully fund the two signature promotions, adding as many smaller promotions as you can afford, you'll create some of your own luck.

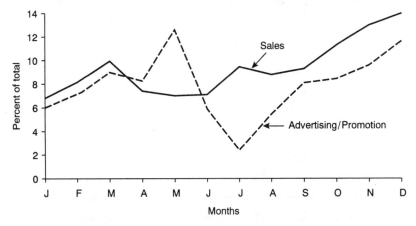

Figure 11-5. A typical sales and advertising curve.

The work sheet for budgeting of your monthly advertising/promotion investment should look like Figure 11-6.

This is how to complete the work sheet:

1. Write monthly sales from the previous year in the first column.
2. Compute the percentage contributed each month to annual sales by dividing the annual sales total into each month's sales. Write the percentage in column 2.
3. Write monthly advertising/promotion costs for last year in column 3.
4. Compute the percentage contributed each month to annual advertising/promotion cost by dividing the annual cost into each month's cost. Place in column 4.
5. Write realistic sales goals for each month for next year in column 5.
6. Fix a percentage to be used each month for advertising/promotion. Use the same percentage for each month. Write in column 6.

| | **Last Year** | | | | **This Year's Sales/Advertising Budget** | | | |
| | Sales | | Advertising/Promotion | | | | | |
	Dollar Amount	Percent of Total	Dollar Amount	Percent of Total	Dollar Amount: Sales	Adv./ Prom. Invest.	Dollar Amt: Advertising/ Promotions	Key Promotions
Jan	❶	❷	❸	❹	❺ X	❻ =	❼	❽
Feb	1,000,000	9.0	42,000	6.2	1,200,000	4.0	48,000	
Mar								
Apr								
May								
June								
July								
Aug								
Sep								
Oct								
Nov								
Dec								
Total								

Figure 11-6. Advertising/promotion budget work sheet.

7. Multiply the budgeted sales goal by the fixed percentage investment (column 5 × 6) for each month. Place the number in column 7. That is what you need to spend on advertising/promotion to hit your sales goal.
8. Note the months for your two signature promotions and other important promotions you want to run.

This is an excellent place to start all your advertising/promotion decisions. The two signature promotions and their timing should be decided before the new year starts. Everything else is fluid. The actual planning and final budgeting of sales and advertising/promotion should be done quarterly, 60 days before the start of the actual quarter.

ADVERTISING/PROMOTION PRINCIPLE 5
Advertising is cumulative—even bad advertising. (Media)

In choosing the best media (TV, radio, etc.) there are two major costs to advertising/promotion: reach (the number of people or households who will see your message) and frequency (the number of times the people or households will see the message). If you want to reach more people or households, the cost increases. If you want to have the message seen more times, the cost increases. Consequently, the Main Street retailer is always trying to balance reach and frequency to get customers to visit the store.

Obviously, if you're not sure who your target markets (pathways) and your core customers are, the tendency is to go for more reach and less frequency. But if you have segmented your market, you will know exactly who you want to reach and you will avoid delivering your message to those who have no interest in your product or service. You will reduce the quantity or reach and allow yourself more frequency, which is critical for the audience to remember your message.

Regardless of the media you use for a promotion, I strongly urge you to choose more frequency.

Each media has a minimum threshold you must achieve if you want interested customers to remember the message and hopefully

Media	Frequency needed to remember
Direct mail	1–2
Newspaper	3
Television	5
Radio	15

Figure 11-7. Number of times a person must hear a message to remember.

respond and visit your store (Figure 11-7). Any promotion should deliver at least these frequencies, depending on media.

Those numbers don't guarantee everyone will remember your message. Even during your most adroit (you have communicated to your core customer and many like them) and fun promotion, a core customer will come in and say, "I didn't know these shoes were on sale. You know they're my favorite shoes. How come I didn't know about the promotion?" Don't despair. Many people are preoccupied with everyday living and precious few live in expectation of your next ad or promotion, except, of course, for your two signature promotions. Most people need to be told, retold, and then reminded what you told them. The cumulative effect of repetition will convince prospective customers to come to your store, or to avoid you because they don't like the message. But the message will get through!

ADVERTISING/PROMOTION PRINCIPLE 6
Advertising is cumulative—even bad advertising.
(Creative or design of ad)

Main Street retailers get bored with their creative approach to their advertising/promotion long before customers do. You become self-critical and want to change the creative, to give it more punch or excitement. Don't do it. Not only must you repeat your message (frequency) many times for the customer to remember, you must be consistent with your creative elements at all times and with all media, otherwise you confuse the customer and the core customers believe you are changing your company direction when you change your creative or ad design.

Consistency will not restrict you. Commit to it and you will build top-of-the-mind awareness.

There is no right look; if your customers like black reverse type (white letters on blackground), then use it regularly. Advertisers consider the look very déclassé, but if your customers respond, who cares what someone else thinks is good-looking? Don't end this look until the customers request it. (One more reason to continue your listen-naively sessions!)

I have listed creative elements that should be consistent and those that you can vary:

MEDIA	CONSISTENT	VARY
Newspaper	All typeface	Use of color.
	Location in ad for:	Size of headline.
	store address,	If you have special
	phone number,	hours, place
	store hours, credit	prominently.
	options, store logo,	
	and slogan.	
	Type of border.	
	Use of white space.	
	Benefit promises.	
	Picture or drawing of	
	products.	
Radio	Spokesperson (should	Remote—radio
	be owner).	station comes to
	Jingle.	your store and
	Type of background	produces show;
	music.	spokespeople are
	Location in	radio personality
	commercial for	and owner.
	store address,	Commercials should
	phone number,	sound like they are
	store hours, slogan.	part of show.

MEDIA	CONSISTENT	VARY
Radio (continued)	Pace and character of presentation.	
TV	Spokesperson (should be owner). Jingle (should be same as radio). Background music (should be same as radio). Location in commercial for store address, phone number, store hours, and slogan. Visuals used. Pace and character of commercial.	Color or black and white.
Direct Mail	Quality and type of envelope and stationery. Quality reproduction and printing. If not letter, all elements of mailing must have the same creative look, from balloons to coupons. Location of store address, phone number, store hours, logo, and slogan should be the same for all letters.	Actual mailing—can be anything.

Take a look at the Abbey Carpet's flexible but consistent creative and graphic look for newspaper advertising (Figure 11-8). The look is versatile and can be used in any size and any type of promotion or sale.

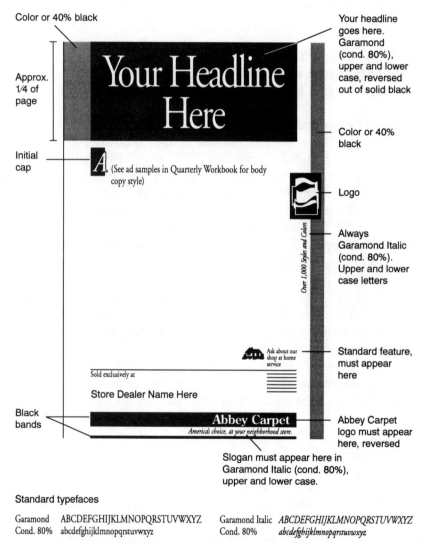

Figure 11-8. Consistent graphic look.

A consistent style in all media will help you create top-of-the-mind awareness. A consistent look will not restrict you. You can be imaginative and daring with a consistent look. The versatility and flexibility of the look is dependent on your creative juices; don't seek another look to stimulate your advertising and promotions. Consistency is not the hobgoblin of small minds—it is essential to smart, effective communication with your customers.

ADVERTISING/PROMOTION PRINCIPLE 7
Media values: If your core customer reads, views, or listens to it, you should advertise/promote with it.

I've often heard Main Street retailers talking about the right media to use. "Is there a right media to use to create traffic in the store?" The response is inevitably, "I like TV, I'm getting good results." Good results are fine, but great results come when you can say, "I know the media my core customers use most often; I even know the parts of the newspaper they read, and what shows they like on TV. That's where they'll see my advertising and promotions." When you listen naively, you will learn this information. If you don't listen naively, you will only guess at the right media to use.

Unless you have a very different-from-average core customer, I think you'll find they have an appetite for more than one medium. They might prefer one, but they will regularly use at least one other. Most promotions should use two media to be sure the message reaches those you have targeted. Nevertheless, each medium has strengths and weaknesses. Some media are more appropriate for certain type promotions and each has an intrinsic marketing value.

Direct Mail

The better you know your core customers, the more you know about where they live. And the better you have listened naively to your core customers, the more response you'll get from direct mail. If you do not complete the task of segmenting, direct mail is a very expensive and low-response advertising method. Don't use direct mail if you haven't segmented your markets. If you have segmented, look at the advantages:

1. *Selectivity.* Unlike any other medium, you can single out and communicate with potential customers by ZIP code or street block, your pin-cluster areas, income, sex, or any way you desire. You don't have to waste your advertising money on sending the message to those who aren't interested. Quality of potential customers (they have certain demographic or lifestyle characteristics similar to your core customers) is more important than quantity. With direct mail, you can choose exactly who will receive your message. No other media can promise that.

2. *Flexible.* There are almost limitless formats with direct mail. If it can be mailed, it can be used by your store. (I once received a coconut mailed to me from a wayward student in Hawaii; the stamp was glued to the coconut.) It is also flexible in the customers to whom you chose to mail. You can add and delete customers, or change your profile altogether and mail to another target market.

3. *It will be seen.* Every piece of mail, regardless of its appropriateness, will be seen for at least four seconds. On average, customers make a four-second decision; they look at the envelope and then either throw it away or open and read whatever you have sent. If you've done the segmentation work and have a strong benefit printed on the envelope, you'll pass the four-second test.

4. *Personal and private.* Mail communication is personal. It is directed at a specific person, by name. Customers control when and how they receive your communication. It can be put aside and read later that day. Delay in reading your message does not mean they are not interested. Actually, it's quite the opposite. If they delay reading your communication, it means they want to give it their undivided attention. However, if they get up and go to the refrigerator during your TV commercial break, that message has vanished forever.

5. *Companion media.* Except for a private sale or a special communication with just your core customers, I would use direct mail with one other traditional medium: It should be mailed when

you're advertising in the other media. More people will pay attention to the mail if they have seen the ad in the newspaper or on TV.

Disadvantages of direct mail:

1. *Expensive.* Direct mail costs more per reader. If you want to announce some great event to the world, direct mail is too expensive. If you have not segmented your target markets, direct mail will be thrown out by most recipients, which increases the cost per reader.
2. *Poor "frequency" media.* It's too expensive, and too frustrating and confusing to your prospective customers, to mail a promotional piece five times. So, unless you're writing your core customers about a secret sale or announcing a private sale for a select group of prospective customers, direct mail should be used with another medium to build frequency.
3. *Junk-mail syndrome.* As more and more people receive more and more unsolicited mail, an automatic reflex motion to the trash occurs. Your promotional piece won't even get the four-second evaluation.
4. *Too complicated.* Direct mail only works if you have segmented your target markets and have planned out four months, have an active database of customers and prospective customers, and have a fulfillment house (a company that addresses and stuffs the envelopes and, if you want, maintains your database) that can complete its task on time at a low cost.

Most retailers fail at direct mail because they haven't segmented their target markets. Like so many things in marketing, if you do the hard work of really knowing your customer, direct mail is easy and inexpensive. Direct mail is a must for your two signature promotions, private sale, and secret sale to your core customers, and it will be an important part of your Keeping Customers program, which will be discussed in the next section.

Newspaper

Historically, newspapers have owned the lion's share of the Main Street retailers' advertising budget. In the past, Main Street retailers even had a price advantage over national advertising by large retailers. Imagine that. The Main Street retailer received the lowest price. However, most newspapers have changed their pricing policy and no longer charge national accounts (Sears, Wal-Mart, etc.) a higher price. That is not good news for the Main Street retailer.

Even with the increased national retail advertising in the newspaper, there are still significant benefits for the Main Street retailer to use newspaper advertising:

1. *Readers enjoy ads in newspapers.* They want to see ads. They consider ads part of the overall information of what's happening in the community. No other media can make this claim. Radio and TV advertising are intrusive and generally unwelcome. People tolerate those ads, but newspaper readers look for and enjoy newspaper ads. (That does not guarantee they will pay attention to your ad or, if they do, that they will like it.)

2. *Good coverage of local marketing area.* Most newspapers have clear circulation strengths. In the areas where they are most successful, three out of four households will receive the paper. If they are strong in the pin-cluster markets for your core customer, three-out-of-four readership is almost as good as direct mail and usually much less expensive.

3. *Lifestyle segments.* Newspapers have become more sophisticated and have created many specific lifestyle segments that are directed at different important target markets the newspaper wants to attract. If you know that senior citizens are a secondary target market (pathway) and the newspaper has a space devoted to such things as senior events, this could be a very good place to run your advertising/promotions. Your newspaper can tell you who reads (not peruses) the different lifestyle sections (seniors, Spanish, teen, gardening, weekend events, travel, etc.).

4. *No creative cost.* Most newspapers have a creative staff who will design your ad for no additional cost. They can help discipline your look and create excitement.

5. *Weekly newspaper.* There are more than 7,000 weekly newspapers in the United States. These papers are read, not perused. There is no hint of national news, but the local news is personal and mostly positive, like who won the raffle at Friday's church bake sale. If your core customer is served by the weekly, and the weekly has solid distribution in your key pin-cluster markets, it's the best media buy for you. Your core customer will read and study your ad, and the cost will be a fraction of direct mail or daily newspaper cost. And unlike the daily newspaper, the weekly newspaper and your advertisement will stay around the house for seven days.

So, why *wouldn't* you use newspaper advertising for your Main Street retail store? Some of the disadvantages are created by societal changes and new technology and cannot be corrected by the newspaper.

1. *Declining circulation.* Fewer people are using a newspaper for information. Turner's *CNN Headline News,* all-news radio stations, and computer on-line programs have become important sources of information for many people. The trend will continue as the next computer-literate generation looks to the computer screen for news and entertainment.

2. *Reading time declining.* Fewer people are purchasing a newspaper and those who do spend less time reading it. (I don't think this is true about the weekly newspaper, which can be read throughout the week.)

3. *National retailers creating clutter.* With the new pricing policy of most newspapers for national retailers, the big retailers are spending more on newspapers, especially on inserts. This dominance makes it harder for the Main Street retailer to get their message across without increasing the frequency and cost to advertise in the newspaper.

Newspapers, however, remain an excellent communication vehicle for the Main Street retailer. Your local newspaper should be part of your two signature promotions and hopefully your press release announcing this unique community event will run as a news item when your ads appear in the newspaper. If you choose a newspaper for most of your advertising/promotions because your core customers read the newspaper, a consistent graphic and visual look, and, if possible, consistent location in the newspaper (sports section, gardening section, etc.) will increase the value of your ads.

Pay special attention to the weekly newspapers in your marketplace. Unfortunately, many have the feel and look of a Pennysaver-type direct-mail piece. But if they are being circulated in your pin-cluster market area, include them in your media plan. Most national retailers don't advertise in the weeklies, so you can make a dominant statement to your core customers for little money.

Radio

Just when radio seemed destined to be one loud rock-and-roll station after another and little else, Americans turned to radio for news, talk, elevator music, sports, and much more. Radio literally came back to life by narrowcasting. There are few general-interest radio stations. Each one of the 8,000 radio stations in the United States has a narrow focus, and like the good retailer, each station is dominant in its niche and they are becoming even more specialized. In the big city, there is a radio station for old-time rock-and-roll, hard rock, heavy metal rock, grunge rock, and four other rocks I don't understand or like. But the good news is that each one of those stations delivers to a unique, well-defined listener. Radio can be a segmenter's dream.

Radio advantages:

1. *Narrowcasting at its best.* This industry's survival depended on the listeners' wish to listen exclusively to only the type of music, talk, sports, or religion that they enjoyed. (As I have mentioned, narrowcasting is fundamental to the success of maga-

zines, radio, TV, retail, and the service industry.) Radio responded and now offers the retailer who has segmented their market an excellent fit of the right radio station for a core customer.

2. *Selling the promotion. Radio is excellent at selling an event or promotion and creating a sense of urgency.* (Never try to promote or sell a product on radio—promote events.) Also, no other media can hype a promotion and create interest the way an on-site (remote) radio show can, especially if you use a local radio personality. (Remotes are more expensive than just running commercials, but plan to use remotes for your two signature promotions.)

3. *Personal.* Unlike any other media, radio builds attachments and loyalties. You can create a personal relationship with listeners. That's why I think the owner should be the radio spokesperson, otherwise radio is not being used to its full potential. (You won't achieve this attachment or personal relationship by just reading creative copy. Think of the personality you want to show your prospective customers and have fun with it.)

4. *Creative.* Much of radio advertising is loud background music and turgid prose but it doesn't have to be that way. When done well, radio advertising is very creative. When it works well, radio advertising demands that the listener do the creative work and fill in the gaps and the visuals. Think of the Motel 6 radio commercials and the signature line, "We'll keep the light on." The commercials were inexpensive, but the listener enjoyed participating in and visualizing the little stories. You can do the same thing.

Radio has two weaknesses:

1. *Combination media.* Use radio with another medium. Don't use radio alone. Hearing, alone, provides the weakest form of retention. It takes more frequency (the number of times one commercial is run) for the listener to remember what you said. (See Figure 11-7 on page 196.) When you use radio in conjunction

with another media, be sure to achieve a high frequency of your message (at least 15 times per week).

2. *Too many radio stations.* The number of radio stations is a double-edged sword. It has allowed narrowcasting, but every radio station seems to claim their core listener is your core customer. Most radio stations have generalized information about their listeners, but few have accurate and useful target market information. *I would avoid any station whose promise is not matched by good research. Stations can afford it. If you can take the time to segment your target markets, they can, too.* Don't buy from a radio station that does not have real, segmented listener markets. Tell them to get smart or get lost, but don't buy a promise.

Radio is best for creating a sense of urgency over a short period of time. It should be part of your two signature promotions with a remote on your best sales day of the promotion. In addition, if you are willing to take some ribbing from your friends, you can create a genuine, fun personality for your store throughout the year. It's okay to be corny, just be real.

TV

For the first 30 years of its existence, TV was made up of three networks (ABC, CBS, NBC). In that period the supply of local stations affiliated with networks has not increased, but the demand for commercial space on TV skyrocketed, and so did the prices for anyone who wanted to advertise on any of the network stations. TV priced itself beyond what most Main Street retailers could afford. Cable changed all that.

For the past 10 years, the network-affiliated stations have lost market share (viewers) to cable. Within the next 10 years, I'm confident that cable will become the dominant TV system and the networks will continue to fade. Cable is TV narrowcasting. That's why cable will dominate. The good news for the Main Street retailer is that cable is affordable and the different cable networks deliver a unique, specific target market for the Main Street retailer who has segmented their market. Let the national retailers worry about the network dinosaurs.

The advantages of TV are:

1. *Sight, sound, motion, color, and soon, maybe, smell.* There is no more powerful medium for advertising than TV. If the viewer doesn't change channels or leave the room, TV can deliver the most memorable advertising message. You're more apt to remember a good (and awful) TV commercial sooner and keep the image in your mind longer than other media.
2. *Excellent for product and promotion.* If you want to demonstrate a new product, TV is the medium to use. TV also can build excitement for your promotion and create a sense of urgency equal to radio.
3. *Reach (network affiliates only).* TV is the most cost-effective media if you want to go for the highest reach (number of households or people). A Main Street retailer should consider network TV for a "going out of business sale." Otherwise, pass and go to cable.
4. *Narrowcasting (cable only).* Cable TV has brought affordable TV advertising to the Main Street retailer, but that price advantage is going to erode as more Americans watch more cable TV. With the continued growth of cable viewership and new cable networks, cable TV will compete with direct mail for delivering a clearly defined audience you can fit with your segmented target markets. For that reason, cable TV is right for the smart Main Street retailer.

The disadvantages of TV are:

1. *Expensive production.* Creating and producing a TV commercial is expensive, whether the commercial is good or not.
2. *Expensive time.* The cost of placing the TV commercial (buying time) on network TV affiliates is beyond the reach of 99% of Main Street retailers. However, this is not so for cable TV.

3. *Refrigerator and bathroom syndrome.* Generally speaking, people try to avoid TV commercials. It does you no good to pay for TV production and carefully choose (and pay dearly for) programs your commercial will run on, and then find out the sofa, wall, and dog were the only things watching.

TV is powerful and expensive. With cable, TV is less expensive and can be very productive for the single-store retailer. Thanks to the narrowcasting of TV, cable TV should be part of your two signature promotions.

ADVERTISING/PROMOTION PRINCIPLE 8
Great advertising/promotion can ruin a mediocre product.

Great advertising/promotion can ruin a mediocre product or store. Indeed. *Think of advertising/promotion as an invitation to a party celebrating a special event.* Far too often, Main Street retailers spend hours fretting about the look and words of the invitation and scant minutes preparing the store and informing the employees about what should happen at the party. The guests are not happy.
Think of advertising/promotion as a promise. Stated or implied in your advertising/promotion piece is a promise of performance. Look at any newspaper advertisement for a Main Street retailer in your town. There are usually at least five promises the retailer makes to the reader. Some, if not all, of these promises appear in most ads:

1. Special price on products
2. Inventory available of these products
3. Friendly store
4. Something new
5. Price guarantee

6. Service guarantee
7. Special hours

Will these promises be kept? Will the store not just meet, but exceed the customers' expectations based on the promises made in the ad?

Advertising/promotion can only invite people to come to your store and it builds expectation of what they will see and how they will be treated. The Main Street retailer must exceed the promise in the store. That's how you create clients and advocates.

Advertising/Promotion Conclusion

Like all other marketing tactics, advertising/promotion succeeds in finding customers in the most productive way when the Main Street retailer has complete knowledge of the customer. When you have segmented your target markets, advertising is less of a mystery and much more cost efficient.

Like all marketing tactics, advertising succeeds with discipline. A disciplined graphic look and a disciplined tone consistently used have a cumulative value. Customers will recognize your look and pay attention to the ad if you are consistent.

Promotions are always better than advertising. Promotions are multidimensional and, if done correctly, will force the Main Street retailer to exceed the customers' expectations.

Advertising/promotion is the method of communicating with prospective customers in the consumer market. You will learn the best type of advertising/promotion when you build your consumer markets.

The three ways to build the consumer market (New Like Old, New Pathway, and New Doors) all use advertising/promotion in different degrees and different ways.

New Like Old

It bears repeating: New Like Old is always the first and best place to start when looking for new customers. It's always easier, smarter, and cheaper to find new customers who behave like your existing customers. And if New Like Old is best, New Like Core is the best of the best.

The loyalty ladder (Figure 11-9) can help demonstrate this marketing approach and the budget needed to build your markets.

Most retailers spend 95% of their marketing budget on general advertising (TV, radio, and newspaper) in an attempt to find new customers, yet spend only pennies on programs to keep customers. You should spend only 70% of your marketing dollars on finding new customers and 30% on keeping customers. (In Section IV, Keeping Customers, you will learn how to create programs to keep customers and also find new customers, all for the same investment.) The trick is to spend the 70% productively. New Like Old is the way to achieve higher productivity for your limited marketing budget.

Listen Naively

Once a month you should sit down with 10 core customers and talk about your business. Do this every month without fail. The goal is the same for the consumer and the business section. You want to enhance your relationship with your core customers so they will become advocates and find new customers for you, and you want their critique (good and bad) of your operation, so you can continually improve in ways that are important to them.

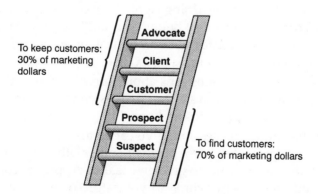

Figure 11-9. Overall marketing budget.

Following are guidelines for the listen naively monthly sessions:

1. Hold the meeting on a Saturday for 1½ hours in the store, before it opens.
2. Give a name to the group (Customers Are Right, It's Your Store, We Try Harder, That's Why We Listen).
3. Invite the customers in a letter. None of this, "Hey, why doncha come down Saturday, and we'll talk . . . ."
4. The session should be informal, with coffee and something to nibble on, but it should be structured. This is not a feel-good session (they'll feel that way because you asked); you need their best critical thinking to help your business prosper.
5. Structure the meeting in four parts: What are we doing right? What are we doing wrong? Are there products or services we should add? Where or how can we find more customers like you?
6. Your employees should participate in the meeting as listeners. Don't argue with the customers. Remember, a customer's perception of reality *is* reality.
7. Pay close attention to convenience factors or customer-service issues. (If any of these types of issues are repeated over six or seven sessions, you need to consider changing.)
8. Use a flip chart and have an employee record the points made. In the "What are we doing right?" session, always ask, "Does the competition do that better than us?" You'll gain a tremendous amount of information about your competition.
9. Have each customer fill out a "Media Use and Lifestyle Sheet." It should include questions about what TV shows they watch regularly, what radio stations they listen to regularly, newspapers they subscribe to, and three favorite leisure activities.
10. At the end of the session, give each participant a modest gift and 10 special Seal-of-Approval coins with your store name. Tell the participants to give one Seal-of-Approval coin to each friend who has not come to your store or has only shopped there on rare occasions. The friend will receive a special discount if they bring in their Seal-of-Approval coin.

11. Take a picture of the group. You should have a prominent wall display of all the monthly groups under whatever name you give them.

There is one difference with the listen naively sessions between business and consumer markets. In the business markets you have few customers. So, after talking to five or 10 businesses in a listen naively session, you will have a very good feel for what the core customer thinks about you.

That is not the case with the consumer market. Ten or 20 customers in the consumer market are not enough to be statistically accurate. They are not representative of all your core customers. You can get a feel for certain issues and some great creative marketing ideas from your customers, but it will take one year of listen naively sessions to be sure that recurring problems or opportunities are significant. It's worth the wait.

What do you get for your efforts? In one year:

1. You will have 120 advocates for your Main Street retail store.
2. These advocates will have given out 1,200 Seal-of-Approval coins to people like themselves.
3. They will have told another 3,000 friends about your commitment to improving your business.
4. You will have received 25 excellent creative suggestions from display to hours open, from your employees' dress to your logo, and from new business opportunities to new product ideas.
5. Your employees, in turn, will be energized. Positive ideas for change will become the rule, and rumors and negative energy will become the exception.
6. You will know what media the core customers use most often, what specific radio stations they listen to, and what TV programs they watch. You also will know their newspaper usage, what sections they read, and which ones they peruse. (This will help you decide what is the best media to use to find more New Like Old prospective customers.)
7. You will know the leisure activities your core customers enjoy. This can be used for creative promotions and also to better understand them as human beings, not just statistics.

8. Finally, you will be absolutely sure about the benefits the core customers think they are receiving when they buy from you. The benefits they are receiving are the answers to: "What are we doing right?"

All this can be done for $500 a year. That $500 investment and 18 hours of listening naively will get you closer to the customer than your competition will be. When you know your customer better than your competition does, you win. All it takes is discipline.

Act Direct

Now you get a chance to use your pin-cluster information and make all that hard work of research and segmentation pay for itself. Special promotions and direct mail will carry the message to your core cluster you have identified. You also will be able to use the information from your listen naively sessions to build more effective general media advertising (TV, radio, and newspaper).

Three distinct actions must occur to make the most out of segmentation. When you complete these actions, you will have found many new customers and created a framework for an intelligent program directed at keeping customers. (That framework will be discussed in the next section, Keeping Customers.) The three distinct actions for Acting Direct and building consumer markets are:

1. Get the names.
2. Create promotions and repeat benefits.
3. Keep the names.

Get the Names   The action starts with names. First, your database (list of customer names, addresses, and, if possible, what they have bought from your store) must include most, if not all, of your customers, regardless of where they live. Second, you must put together the names and addresses of all the potential customers who live in your core pin-cluster areas. (See pages 159–162.) The best way to achieve this is to purchase a reverse directory for your trading area. (Any bookstore can order it for you.) A reverse directory organizes people by street, then by name. List all the streets in your pin-cluster area, go to the reverse directory, and input into your computer all the names of the people who live on those streets. Be sure to list all the streets, even if no one has bought from you on specific streets. If a street is within the cluster boundary, the names of all the people are included. They will be listed in order of address:

Jenkins Way
1402   Williams, James
1404   Smith, Joe
1406   Jones, Jimmy

When you input these data into your computer, indicate who is an existing customer. Even in your best pin cluster, you probably don't sell to more than 5% of all the people living in that area. So, by this calculation, you will have a list of potential customers (who are like your best customers), that is 20 times larger than your list of existing customers.

Using the reverse directory and inputting all these names into your computer is time consuming. Another way to acquire the information is to buy the names from a list broker. You don't actually buy these names, you rent the names for one mailing. Since you want to mail to these New Like Old prospective customers more than once, it becomes far too expensive to rent the list every time you want to do a mailing. (If you try to use it a second time, without paying, the list broker will send an enforcer to your Main Street retail store to punish you. They will know you have mailed your message a second time because they seed the list with fake names that come back to the list broker, so don't be tempted to misbehave.) You want full control of your database. Build it the old-fashioned way, with hard work, and you can keep the names for as long as you want.

Create Promotions   I hope I've made my case for promotions over traditional, one-dimensional advertising. A well-executed promotion will involve your employees and if you have good, concerned employees, they will make sure your store is ready for the event. Advertising alone rarely elicits employee involvement, therefore nothing special happens other than selling products at a low gross profit.

If you have completed the consumer segmentation for your Main Street retail store, and have a map of your trading area with the pin cluster completed, direct mail is the most productive media you can use.

When you deliver mail to *all* your existing customers and to prospective customers exclusively in the pin-cluster geography (those areas where your core customers live), you dramatically increase the likelihood of talking to a consumer who is interested in your product or service. Your message will be read, not discarded. Direct mail is the best medium to capitalize on your valuable segmenting information.

For all promotions directed at New Like Old prospective customers, you should use direct mail and one other medium. (Remember, you can't build frequency with direct mail; the other media will do that and hopefully attract New Like Old prospective customers who are living outside your pin-cluster marketing areas.) The correct companion medium is the one the core customers use most. (You learned which media they used most from your listen naively sessions.)

For the two signature promotions, spend all your advertising (media) budget on direct mail (to all existing customers and prospective customers in the key pin-cluster areas), the companion media, and remote radio broadcast from your store. For all other promotions you run throughout the year, commit the largest share of your budget to attracting more New Like Old prospective customers into your Main Street retail store.

Benefits   In many cases, one of the key benefits for your promotion will be a savings story. That is fine, but you should always include the benefits your customers have told you are important to them. Always. *Constantly repeating those things you do exceptionally well will help position your company so that more customers like your existing customers will come to your store. Don't advertise new benefits you think someone might like. Keep the benefits your customers have told you are important and repeat them to anyone who will listen.*

A few suggestions on benefit statements:

1. Choose no more than five benefits. Your core customers have told you these benefits are the reasons they buy from you and not from your competition.
2. Use very few words to describe each benefit. Do not imitate. If every store in town has the "lowest price, guaranteed," no one has the lowest price.
3. These benefits should be included in all ads and media. You may weave the benefits into the ads and commercials, but you also should include them at the end of the TV or radio commercial. For newspapers, include them at the bottom near your store name and address. For direct mail, include them near your name and address on the envelope and letterhead.
4. When the customer comes into your store, those same benefits should be displayed on signs around the store, on employee badges, on all brochures, and on all invoices. They should be reflected in the demeanor of all employees, and the salesperson should remind the customer of these benefits.
5. Never fail to keep your benefit promises.

Marketing Principle 3 says, "Marketing is discipline: creating a few meaningful benefits (better than the competition) directed at specific customer groups." The discipline is not just choosing a few benefits, the discipline also is repeating the same benefits in every form of customer contact and communication, over and over again, until you and your employees could scream. But don't scream and don't stop.

Keep Names   This Keep Names action is the last step in finding new customers and, at the same time, the first step in keeping customers. Regardless of the media used to attract the customer, you must begin to collect the names of your customers (those who buy from you) so that you can complete the promise of smart marketing: to find and keep customers. After you segment your markets and devise great promotions to build markets, you want to know the names of your new customers so you can communicate with them in special ways. This is one way you move the customer up the loyalty ladder. By communicating regularly, you will exceed their expectations and create clients and advocates for your Main Street retail store.

In Chapter 10, Segmenting Markets, I discussed the need to try to get the names and addresses of your customers. If you sell many small-ticket items and you think you will irritate your customer with slower service as you write down all this information, you must devise another way to build a customer list. I suggest the following:

1. Have a drawing for buying customers only. Have them fill out an entry form while you ring up the sale.
2. Set up a small display area with the sign, "If you give us your name and address, we'll save you time and money." Explain that they'll receive a newsletter, special promotion, or whatever.
3. Set up a small display area with the sign, "We're not as big as McDonalds; we like to know who our customers are, not how many."

Getting and keeping the names of those who buy from you is vital to knowing your customer better than your competition does. However you get the names of your customers, be sure your employees use the method consistently. Knowing the general area where customers live is better than not knowing but guessing. Knowing the names and addresses of the largest percentage of your buying customers is the ultimate marketing step.

Trivia Carpets by Trivers

Trivers completed his segmentation and pin-cluster analysis. Figure 11-10 shows what he found:

His core customers live in two distinct and separate areas

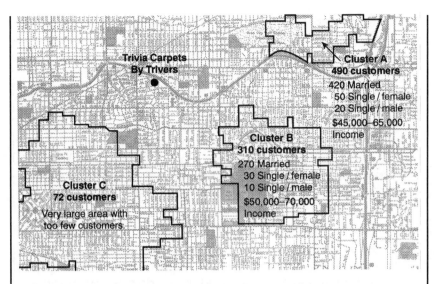

Figure 11-10. Location, sex, and income of customers.

(clusters A and B). He was ready to Act Direct. One of his network of business friends told Trivers of his success with a private sale. Trivers's friend sent him all the promotional material he had used, and Trivers took the ideas he liked and added others his employees thought would create a powerful promotion.

This is what they put together:

1.   They purchased the Polk Reverse Directory (Polk is the company that offers the reverse directory in Trivers's area).

2.   It took 40 hours to input all the names for the two core areas. In clusters A and B, Trivers has 800 buying customers and 15,300 prospective customers.

3.   Since Trivers records all purchases on sales slips with a name and address, he separated customers (those who have purchased from his store) from prospective customers.

4. He created two letters (one to existing customers and one to prospective customers), using the same Private Sale theme but he changed the greeting and one sentence in the body of the letter to better personalize it. The existing customer's greeting read, "We appreciate your recent purchase from our store and would like you to be our guest at a very special three-hour event." For the prospective customer, the greeting read, "Many of your neighbors have purchased flooring from us in the last year and they have suggested we offer a Private Sale for select homeowners. This very special three-hour event. . . ."

5. Trivers promised discounts from 20% to 40% on selected items; first-time viewing of new imported tile from Italy with a representative from the company; employees, including the installers, dressed in tuxedos; demonstrations of the High Five benefits you only receive from Trivia Carpets; meetings with members of the Carpet Council who were the last customers to participate in the listen naively sessions; a drawing at the end of the night for a weekend in a nearby bed-and-breakfast; champagne; hors d'oeuvres; local high school jazz combo; balloons; and refrigerator magnets with the High Five benefits and Trivia Carpets logo.

6. The High Five benefits were shown throughout the store and became a permanent part of all communication and display from that point on. These benefits came from the listen naively sessions with core customers.

7. When the customers arrived, they were asked to write down the names of friends who might be interested in floor covering. Each customer's name was put in the drawing drum for the bed-and-breakfast weekend. The more friends customers thought of, the better the chance of winning. (The atmosphere at the store that night was so enjoyable and professional that many people who did not buy gave names of prospective customers. Trivers added 800 names to his prospective customer file.)

8. In addition to the representative from the Italian tile company, there were manufacturer representatives from four carpet and wood companies. That was very smart. People love to talk to the pros, and Trivers needed these people to help write orders.

9. No TV. No radio. No newspaper.

10. Trivers made a very modest mailing of 16,100, but to the right people—quality not quantity, all based on the segmentation work and the resulting pin cluster.

The private sale for Trivia Carpets by Trivers was a smashing success. Existing customers appreciated the invitation. New customers were impressed. No ad, in fact, no three ads had ever drawn as many people and created as much business. Trivers now understands the common sense of pin clustering, the value of direct mail, and the power of creating promotions.

New Pathway

If the subtitle for the New Like Old marketing process could be "Ready, Aim, Fire," the subtitle for the New Pathway marketing process is "Ready, Fire, Aim." With the New Like Old segmenting and pin-cluster work, you know you are aiming right at your target market. But with the New Pathway, you're going to fire (advertise) first and hope you hit the new target market (pathway). It won't be efficient or very accurate, but it is the way to try to reach a customer group that has not paid much attention to your Main Street retail store. I'm reminded of the TV stunt which is followed by, "Don't try this at home."

My caution to you is: Don't go after another target market just to break the boredom and do something different. Only go after a new target market if you are convinced they seek the same benefits (with modest alteration) that you are presently delivering to your core customer, and if they are substantial enough to warrant the marketing investment in time and advertising/promotion dollars.

What you really want to do is to see if, in fact, there is a substantial target market (pathway) that is receptive to your message. You do not have the time or the money for a full-fledged, all-out marketing effort to penetrate this new target market. You want to invest no more than 10% of your advertising/promotion funds in this effort. You will probe the market only, nothing more. If there is a target market (pathway) that begins to respond to your message, the results of their response will show up on your annual segmenting and pin-cluster work. It will become a secondary market and you will treat the target market as New Like Old and include it in all your promotions.

Basically, this 10% investment you are making is an active customer research project that should pay for itself in sales from some of those customers you have targeted.

Listen and Guess Naively

How do you guess naively? First, you must question your employees and network of business friends from other cities about potential new target markets (pathways). Listen naively. The shared business wisdom of employees and friends should help you determine if there is another target market (pathway) that is substantial and not currently buying from you. Hopefully, one of your business friends serves this target market in their market area and can tell you if the benefits this market seeks are compatible with the benefits you are presently offering to your core customer.

This is helpful guidance, not real research, but it will suffice. Based on this advice, you must guess naively or call upon your entrepreneurial skills for a feel of the marketplace. If you think there is a fit between your core customer and this new customer group, commit 10% of your advertising/promotion budget for this group for one full year.

Act Pretty Direct

You can't act direct since you don't know your prospective target market. You have some educated guesses as to who they are, how and where they live, and why they buy the way they do, but they are only guesses. So the best you can expect from your message (benefits offered) and media used is to be pretty direct or pretty close to what they want to hear and where they want to hear or see the message. Pretty close works in hand grenades and horse-shoes and it will work for this new target market. If and when the customers respond, they will form a pin cluster and become a secondary target and will be treated as New Like Old for future promotions.

Some guidelines for your New Pathway marketing effort:

1. Do not use direct mail. Direct mail does not work when you are only close to knowing your target market. It will be very expensive and inefficient.
2. Use a general medium other than the companion medium you are using with direct mail for your core customer. If you believe your new target customer (pathway) uses the same general media as your core customer, and they prefer this media, you should not follow this suggestion. But if you think they like and use two media, use the one that you are not using for your core customer.
3. Slightly alter the style and feel of the ads or commercials. Restate the benefits in words that the new target market uses. Remember, when you speak in the idiom of the customers, they will listen.
4. The commercial or ad should not be radically different from your other advertising to your core customer. It must look, sound, feel, and smell like your other advertising. The style should be the same; the words and visuals are different to gain the attention of this new target market.
5. Do not include this effort in your two signature promotions. Take 10% out of the budget for all other promotions and use it just for this new target market.

Keep Names

Keeping the names is a must for your Main Street retail store. Keeping the names of a new target market (pathway) that you are trying to bring to your store is a *double must*. Otherwise, you'll never know if you have created enough interest to warrant a complete commitment and include them in the New Like Old promotion program.

Seeking out new customer groups (pathways) is an important part of Main Street retail marketing. You should not flit from one customer group to another. Decide each year if there is one new target market (pathway) that you believe is substantial enough (lots of people with money) and compatible with your core customer. Constantly communicate (promotion/advertising) to this group for one year. If you are right, they will begin to respond, and will form their own pin cluster large enough to warrant them being treated as New Like Old for future promotions.

New Door

This is the last way to build markets. This takes a broader view than advertising or communication. As in the business market, looking at broad product markets (doors) you are not serving is an important way to feed opportunities and build markets. In most cases, the consumer market of your retail store changes much more often, and more quickly than the business side, so the need to analyze these business opportunities is more important for the consumer market. But you should not make this review on the run. Pull back and annually analyze at least one important business opportunity.

The three questions you must ask about any business opportunity are:

1. Will our core customers benefit from this new business opportunity?
2. Will another customer group that is compatible with my core customers, but who I have been unable to get to buy from me, benefit from this new business opportunity?
3. Can I make a profit from this investment within one year?

When reviewing other broad product markets (doors) you are not serving, the first thing to consider is your core customer. Will this new product market enhance your relationship with your existing core customers? If the answer is Yes (Ask your customers, don't guess), you must give the new market serious consideration. If you would create a whole new core customer who would want different benefits than you are presently offering, you should pass.

Listen Naively

Again, some trustworthy market research is in order. Contact your business friends who operate outside your marketing area to see if any of them are participating in this broad product market (door) that you are considering as a new business opportunity. If one of your friends is now serving this market, visit their store and try to learn everything about how it works and what benefits the customers believe they are receiving from this new business.

If at all possible, sit down with 10 customers of your friend's store who are using this broad product market. The questions you want answered are the same ones you asked when you considered a business opportunity for your business market:

1. Are they like your core customers?
2. If not, would they be compatible with your core customers?
3. Are the benefits they seek from this broad product market (door) similar to those that your store offers?

If you are satisfied with the compatibility or fit of this customer group with your core customer, you should next sit down with 20 of your own core customers, and try to find out:

1. Are they presently buying this program or service from someone else?
2. If so, what does the competition do right? What does it do wrong?
3. Would they buy it from you if you offered it? Why?

By talking to 20 core customers you will get a feel for what customers will expect from your new business venture, but it's not statistically valid. Even if all 20 customers love your idea, it does not mean all your customers will use the new marketing program. Go to your database and send a simple questionnaire to all your customers. If you receive back a minimum of 180 responses, you will have an accurate view of your customers' responsiveness to your new business venture. Here are some suggestions:

1. Use one side, single page, no more than 10 questions.
2. Start with, "Dear Valued Customer: I need your help." (Get right to the point.) The note should be one short paragraph, explaining your new business opportunity. Questions follow. Sign your note.
3. Make the questions answerable with a Yes or a No, and fill in the blanks. Examples: Do you use this service? If not, would you use this service from our company? How often would you use this service from our company?
4. If you're concerned about response rate, make the questionnaire part of a drawing for a modest gift. Customers must mail it in within two weeks to participate. This is the best way to get maximum responses in the least amount of time.
5. Include a stamped, self-addressed envelope. It should be mailed back to your store.
6. Promise your customers that you will let them know the results and what you plan to do. Whether you decided to get in the new business or not, staying in touch with customers is a courtesy they will appreciate. It takes some time, little money, and discipline.

If you received positive responses to your questions, complete a pro forma profit and loss to see if this new venture will pay for itself (pay back the investment you made) in one year. If so, get moving!

Act Direct

If ever there was an opportunity to utilize fully the power of your established database, this is it. The opening of a new broad product market (door) should be treated with the same excitement as open-ing a new store. Consider these promotional ideas for your new business opportunity:

1. Create an inexpensive tri-fold, two-color brochure (8½" × 11" paper folded to make three panels) explaining this new product market. Regardless of how technical or complex your product or service might seem, be sure to use customer words, not industry jargon, to explain this new program that you're offer-ing customers.

2. Prior to your public grand opening, send a direct-mail piece to *all* your existing customers for a private presentation.

3. Give every customer who comes to your after-hours private presentation five brochures and two refrigerator magnets which have your store name and information about your new broad product market (door). Ask them to give four brochures and one magnet to friends.

4. One week later, invite all the *prospective* customers in your pin-cluster area (areas). Do not invite customers. Again, give each prospective customer five brochures and two magnets. Ask them to give four brochures and one magnet to friends.

5. Now you're ready for the public announcement of your new business opportunity. Send a press release to all media.

6. Announce this new program in the newspaper at the same time that it runs the press release. (Even if your usual companion medium is not a newspaper, use a newspaper with your com-panion medium. People look to the newspaper for these types of announcements.)

7. Make this new program part of all your promotions and adver-tising for at least one year. Always mention this program in your direct-mail pieces and all commercials and ads. (Remem-ber, people need to be reminded, re-reminded, and told again before they understand you have something new.)

It's not enough just to fling open the door for your new busi-ness opportunity. You must build awareness of your program. The easiest and smartest place to start to build awareness and sales is with satisfied customers. They are more apt to pay attention to your program sooner than a noncustomer, and obviously more apt to create sales for the program. The second-best customer is New Like Old, but for any customer group, frequency (repetition) is critical. Even after a year of hammering home the point that you have something new, a good repeat customer will walk in and say, "Gee, I didn't know you offered this, when did you decide to get into this business?" Smile, take deep breaths, and give the customer five brochures. The customer now knows about your program and will become your client and advocate.

Keep Names

Keep the names of the customers who use your new program, and include what they purchased in your database. Don't minimize the importance of this information.

Remember the story of my friend who owned a bookstore and spent all her marketing dollars on postcards to customers telling them that a new book arrived? Since she tracked their purchases, she knew which customers loved science fiction (customers have a core reading subject) and informed only the science-fiction aficionados of the new science-fiction arrival. She did the same thing for 11 other subjects. She spent no money on general advertising. These postcards could only be used through a commitment to an active database.

Marketing starts with customers. Finding and keeping customers starts with knowledge of who your customers are and what they buy. That knowledge becomes your database. It is the marketing heart of all Main Street retailers.

Trivia Carpets by Trivers

Trivers had been reluctant to consider opening any new doors (broad product market) to his business. In fact, he used the argument of narrowcasting for the reason not to consider any new business opportunities (doors). He said, "Isn't the idea of narrowcasting directly opposite to your suggestion that I consider a new business opportunity?" I told Trivers the answer is, "Yes, and a little bit of No."

Narrowcasting is a must for most Main Street retailers. They don't have a wide-enough assortment or deep-enough inventory in their core items, and they have too many of the items that customers don't want. Also, most Main Street retailers participate weakly or dabble in smaller broad product markets. They have not committed to these broad product markets (doors) and the customers respond accordingly. Trivers has had unused products and dabbled in some broad product markets (doors). As he gets out of those problems, he will see that there is room fiscally (with inventory and marketing dollars) and physically (with space) for expansion into new broad product markets (doors).

Narrowcasting and new business opportunities are not mutually exclusive. If you practice narrowcasting and let the customers guide you to new business opportunities, you'll be known as the Marketing Swami of Main Street.

Somewhat convinced, Trivers decided to take a close look at carpet cleaning as a door (broad product market) to new sales and profits. Over the years, he didn't give much credence to the recurring complaint, "Why aren't you in the carpet-cleaning business?" He would tell his customers that there were too many carpet-cleaning companies in town and that he really didn't want the hassle. He would recommend a good friend who did a great job. Then the largest local bank, with 14 branch offices, made a proposal: "We will buy replacement carpet from your store every seven years for each branch if you will professionally clean the carpet on a regular schedule." Suddenly, carpet cleaning became a great idea, not just a hassle.

But what about the consumer side? He remembered the consumer complaints, but he didn't know if they constituted real demand or just four customers complaining and no one else caring. But the potential of one new business opportunity opening a new door of sales and profits from the consumer market and a new door of sales and profit from the business market was an opportunity Trivers had to analyze closely.

He decided to do some basic research. Most manufacturers' reps told him it was a dumb idea. Trivers kept wondering: How dumb can the idea be if my largest customer wants the service and some consumers have asked me to offer carpet cleaning? Trivers called Bill Bane, president of Bane-Clene in Indianapolis, Indiana. Bane-Clene manufactured and sold carpet-cleaning equipment. Bill told Trivers he was not the only floor-covering retailer who was finally listening to the customer and not following blindly what the carpet industry was saying. The carpet-cleaning industry association completed awareness research on a regular basis and gave the research to member cleaners. Bill cited the most recent survey. Consumers were asked: "Why did you choose the specific company to clean your carpet?" According to Bill Bane, 50% of the consumers chose the carpet cleaner *after* they had called the carpet store that had installed the carpet and asked for a recommendation. Trivers realized that this happened all the time at his store. He also realized that if he and his people had been listening naively, they would have realized the customer really wanted the response to be, "Yes, we are committed to serving our customers after the sale; we would love to clean your carpet!"

Since none of Trivers's retail friends were in the carpet-cleaning business, he asked Bill for the names of retailers who had been in this business for at least a year. He visited one of the stores and studied the operation, learned how it had to function to be profitable, and went on five carpet-cleaning jobs with the technician. He was now ready to talk to his core customers.

Trivers talked with three different groups of core customers, a total of 20 people. He found that there were two different broad product markets (doors) for cleaning—do-it-yourself and professional cleaning. Those who preferred professional cleaning said they would use Trivia Carpets, but they would not pay a premium. In other words, his operation had to be competitive with existing companies.

Since Trivers had been building a database of existing and prospective customers, he mailed a simple one-page questionnaire, with a self-addressed, stamped envelope, to all existing customers. The response was overwhelmingly in favor of Trivia Carpets by Trivers entering the professional carpet-cleaning business. That's exactly what he did.

Would you go to the trouble of visiting a store to see how it is operating a business that you're considering for expansion? Would you sit down with 20 customers to get a feel for their response? If you had 500 customer names, would you send a questionnaire to all your customers to try to determine what percentage would use your service? Is all that really necessary? Yes! That's how you reduce the risk, increase the probability of success, and get guidance from your existing customers. It's very smart marketing.

BUILDING MARKETS: THE FINAL BUDGET

Your budget for building markets consists of the monthly work sheet for advertising/promotion (see Figure 11-6 on page 194) and

	Last Year				This Year's Sales/Advertising Budget			
	Sales		Advertising/Promotion					
	Dollar Amount	Percent of Total	Dollar Amount	Percent of Total	Dollar Amount: Sales	Adv./ Prom. Invest.	Dollar Amt: Advertising/ Promotions	Key Promotions
Jan	52,000	4.0	2,000	5.1	52,000	3.2	1,664	
Feb	61,000	4.7	2,000	5.1	65,000	3.2	2,080	Private sale preceding public sale
Mar	117,000	9.0	2,500	6.4	140,000	3.2	4,480	
Apr	88,000	6.8	3,000	7.7	92,000	3.2	2,944	
May								
June								
July								
Aug								
Sep								
Oct								
Nov								
Dec								
Total								

Figure 11-11. Advertising/promotion budget work sheet.

key promotion work sheet. See how Trivers has put together his budget for building markets.

Trivers started with the advertising/promotion work sheet (Figure 11-11). For this example, I have completed four months; you should complete it for the entire year and fine-tune it on a quarterly basis.

Trivers is not going to do any advertising/promotion in January, so he will run his first promotion in February and budget January and February's investment for the first promotion. See promotion work sheet (Figure 11-12).

The actual media placement will be completed closer to the promotion date. Budgeting does not ensure a successful promotion. Budgeting requires you to think about this important investment. With this simple two-step promotion budget, you will use your limited resources more wisely and produce more sales.

Conclusion: Finding Customers

Finding customers starts with a thorough knowledge of your core customers and the benefits they seek from your Main Street retail store. The Main Street retailer has the unique ability to understand

Private Sale Preceding Public Sale

Budget

$3,744	Jan./Feb. Budget
3,384	New Like Old
400	New Pathway
—	New Door

Budget Specifics		Direct Mail	+	Newspaper	+	In-store Material
New Like Old	$3,384 =		+		+	
New Pathway	$400 =		+	N/A	+	N/A

Creative Statement:

Figure 11-12. Promotion work sheet.

their customers. It is in their grasp to do so, but precious few take the time. "Kinda knowing my customer" has been good enough so far, why change? The marketplace has changed dramatically, and to win the tug-of-war for customers, the Main Street retailer must understand their customer better than the competition.

You'll never have more inventory than Home Depot, lower prices than Wal-Mart, or be more convenient than Spiegel catalog, but you can know your customers better than all three. That's the way to finding more customers.

One of the great sins in marketing is to pay lip service to knowing your customer, and then spend all your time buying product and advertising. The Main Street retailer will tell me, "Okay, I know my target market, that's not the problem. I just want to know if my newspaper ad should be above the fold and to the right? Is that the best placement in the newspaper?" The real problem is not advertising nor any myriad marketing tactics. Businesses fail for lack of customers and the failure stems from a lack of knowledge about the core customer.

David Ogilvy, the guru of modern advertisers, said, "A blind pig can sometimes find truffles, but it helps to know that they are found in oak forests."

GETTING DOWN TO BUSINESS

Applying Marketing Principles to Your Business

BUILDING MARKETS AND CREATING BENEFITS
Building sales by finding more customers like the ones you have, seeking new target markets (pathways), and creating new business opportunities (doors).

Following is a checklist for building your markets:

Building Business Markets

1. Set a goal: Sign up five New Like Old business customers for the most important broad product markets (doors).

2. Use a listen-naively session and disciplined Act Direct presentation to achieve your goal.
3. Once a year, evaluate a business opportunity you are not participating in. Visit a friend who is in the broad product market.

Building Consumer Markets

1. Set up a database of buying and prospective customers.
2. Set up monthly listen-naively sessions with 10 core customers.
3. Establish an advertising/promotion budget using a fixed percentage for each month.
4. Create two signature promotions. Make them very big.
5. With customer direction, decide on five benefits that become your image—your store's reason for being. Implement the communication of these benefits throughout the company.

IV

KEEPING CUSTOMERS

12

KEEPING CUSTOMERS: THREE BEST WAYS

Keeping customers requires caring more about the customer during and after the sale than your competition does. Keeping customers is about *underpromising* in the commercial or newspaper ad and *overperforming* in the store. (That's a nice surprise.) Keeping customers is not about suddenly responding to the threat of losing customers to the big, new store arriving in town. Keeping customers is about creating an active program in which you and your employees say "Thank you" in many different ways, and the customer says "You're welcome, and I can't wait to tell my friends what a nice time I had." Keeping customers is about moving your existing customers up the loyalty ladder (Figure 12-1) to become advocates for your business.

Ultimately, keeping customers is first about knowing who your core customers are and what benefits they seek from you. Without that basic knowledge, your efforts will be neither personable nor believable since there is no one-size-fits-all program for building customer trust.

Keeping customers takes money, employee training, and discipline. Your program for keeping customers works only if you believe that the real difference between all retailers and service businesses is how you treat your customers, and that marketing wisdom always comes from listening naively to the customer, not to the industry or the genius of the owner. Any Main Street retail store that embraces this retail philosophy will never be accused of customer indifference, which is the major reason for losing a customer.

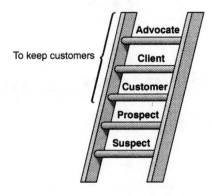

Figure 12-1. Customer loyalty ladder.

This entire section is devoted to keeping consumers, not business customers, due to their large number and complexity. That does not suggest that you should not have a simple, disciplined program in your business market. You should. Use some of my consumer suggestions for the business market as well. In this section, I will start by discussing retail poisons you should avoid at all cost. All your fine efforts to find new customers will be for naught if you are guilty of allowing any of these things to happen in your store. They are poison, and they can be fatal to a good retail operation. I have used the international sign for "Stop, you're doing something wrong," and have subtitled the next chapter Delusions of Adequacy.

The rest of this section on keeping customers is devoted to programs to build your customer trust and create more advocates for your store:

Don't Be Overserviced.

Act Direct. Be Direct.

13

AVOID AT ALL COSTS: DELUSIONS OF ADEQUACY

Betsy Sanders, a former senior Nordstrom executive, talks about how easy it is to learn good retail tactics and service. She says in her book, *Fabled Service*, "One of the reasons that the retail industry provides a fertile ground for learning about the basics of service is that it is so transparent to customers. Thus, you can observe what works and doesn't work from your personal perspective as a customer, then apply these learnings to your own business." Basically, that's what I did with my evaluation (Trivers retail meter) of the new forms of retail. First, I was a customer, and second, a retail observer. You should do the same.

This chapter takes a look at those things the big stores do poorly, because of their bigness, and that you want to be sure you do very well. It also looks at those things many Main Street retailers do poorly out of ignorance or laziness and that you want to do well. The worst kind of business self-deception is to allow your store to be adequate and not special because the big guys don't do it very well and everybody shops there, so why should you worry about it? Nor should you accept (I guarantee it's not acceptable to your customers) displays, signage, warranties, salespeople's behavior, pricing, and advertising in your store that you would not like in a business from which you want to buy. This chapter will help you eliminate any of those retail poisons that can quietly ruin all your efforts to create advocates for your business. Remember, to be competitive means to win the race, not to tie. If you rid your Main Street retail store of any and all of these retail poisons, you will win the race—big time!

○ DELICATESSEN MARKETING

To paraphrase Saddam Hussein, delicatessen marketing is the mother of all retail poisons. It occurs far too often with the Main Street retailer. The Main Street retailer who practices delicatessen marketing has a little bit of this, more of that, and not a whole lot of anything. It's a store in search of a core customer and core products.

If knowing your core customer is essential to finding new customers, committing to a wide assortment and deep inventories of your core products is basic to keeping customers. Marketing Principle 5 says, "People with similar taste, values, and demographics buy similar things . . . usually." Your core customers buy the same products and you must do everything to make them happy.

Invariably, with delicatessen marketing, the retailer has a fairly limited assortment of the core products and runs out of inventory on many of these items. But that doesn't mean the retailer has a small overall inventory for the store. It's just in the wrong places, supporting all the other products the customer has no interest in. It is expensive to support delicatessen marketing with a large part of the inventory sitting on the shelves, and the fast-selling core items regularly out of stock.

The other problem with delicatessen marketing is that the store does not maintain a single point of view.

This can seem very subjective, but a retail point of view is part of the character of the store that distinguishes it from any other, and the point of view must be maintained throughout the store. Continuity or consistency of look in advertising, signage, display, pricing, salespeople presentation, and products creates an image or point of view. With delicatessen marketing, the point of view gets blurred, the customer becomes confused, and the core customer becomes uncomfortable with the mixed signals.

To avoid the poison of delicatessen marketing, bias your marketing for the core products. By so doing, you won't give equal treatment to product assortment or inventory.

First, look at your core products. Do you have the widest assortment possible? Can you expand sizes, colors, or other similar products at different price points? If yes, do so. Then build an inventory and replenishment plan so that you will never run out of these products. Only when you have completed this do you look at products closely related to your core products. If you build your product assortment from the core out, as I have described, you will naturally force many of the unsold products (remnants of delicatessen marketing) off your shelf and into the discontinued bin for final liquidation. With the commitment to core products, you won't have any money for more of these nonproductive products.

When you build the product assortment from the core out and never run out of core items, your store will have taken the correct antidote for the delicatessen marketing poison.

⊘ "YOU MEAN TO TELL ME I DROVE ALL THIS WAY TO YOUR STORE FOR THIS ADVERTISED ITEM, AND YOU DON'T HAVE ANY?"

A Target store manager told me that Target's newspaper advertising inserts carried one-half the items that Kmart or Sears would have included in the same-size advertising piece. The reason was a very important customer benefit: convenience. Target's goal was never to run out of any advertised item for the duration of the promotion, and it knew it couldn't keep that promise by offering twice as many items. All the Target manager had to do was shop at Sears and Kmart to see how unworkable their programs were.

Target decided to be different and always have stock of fewer advertised items while Sears, Montgomery Ward, department stores, Kmart, and many Main Street retailers struggled to maintain stock of numerous advertised items. The problem, for some, was so acute that they began to run out of rain-check slips. I believe this commitment to stock availability for advertised items has helped Target build loyal customers. Even if Target doesn't have the lowest price, customers know the item will be in stock when they respond to the ad. That is very convenient. Returning two weeks later to get the advertised item is very inconvenient.

Main Street retailers should not view this out-of-stock issue like this: "Well, we had 75% of our items in stock, that's pretty good." They should view this issue the way the customers do: Out-of-stocks are inconvenient and totally unacceptable. The Main Street retailers should look at the problem one way only, "How would the customer want it?" If they ask that question, and resolve to give the core customers what they want, they'll keep their core customers and build advocates, just as Target has.

When convenience is one of the key benefits your core customers seek, follow the Target lead.

If price reduction is an important part of your promotions, use core items and buy additional quantities to support the event. Promote only as many items as you can afford to support with additional inventory dollars. Fill out your event offerings with unadvertised specials professionally marked in your store. You can pull unadvertised specials off the promotion anytime without disappointing your customer.

◎ RETAILER INDIFFERENCE

The Number-1 reason Main Street retailers fail to keep customers is due to what the customers perceive as retailer indifference: They feel they are not being treated the way they would like. It is rarely one problem or one occasion that causes customers to forever leave the retailer. Most customers forgive and forget those occasional problems.

Retailer indifference, in the customers' mind, is cumulative. This is a customer's worst nightmare: They call for information, the phone rings 11 times before being answered, and immediately they are put on hold for three minutes. They get the information requested, rush into the store, wait seven minutes for service, then talk to the salesperson who knows nothing about the product they want to buy, only to discover it is out of stock and won't be available for a month. All this retail indifference was experienced during one lunch hour—the only time the customer had to make this purchase. Sadly, that happens all the time.

Most customers view the previous scenario as one of indifference, not incompetence. The customers assume the retailer has the programs in place to run their business professionally, blame the frontline employees for not caring or knowing, and punish the store by not returning. Most of these people are "nice" customers and never complain to the retailer, but bad-mouth the store to all their friends.

I take a different view. The Main Street retailer who allows this to happen is incompetent. It is their responsibility to train, retrain, and train again all their employees. Any Main Street retailer who is too busy to train their people is spending their time on the wrong things.

Marketing Principle 2 says, "Marketing is part of every employee's job." That should not be viewed as a public-relations ploy with all gloss and no substance. It must be practiced every day:

1. The phone should be answered by the third ring, every time. If salespeople are busy, someone else must answer it, including the bookkeeper, stock boy, or owner.

2. Any customer who asks for the owner should not be deferred. No business meeting is more important than a customer.

3. Don't waste money on "on hold" recording services. No customer should be put on hold for more than 10 seconds.

4. Answer all customer calls with, "Hi, this is (your name), how can I help you?" Close all calls with, "Thanks for calling (store name)." Everybody should start and end any phone conversation with customers or vendors this same way.

5. Customers should be acknowledged when they come into the store, even if the salesperson is with someone else. Start with, "Welcome to (your store)."

6. No employee should walk through the store with their head down. Regardless of their position with the company, employees should say, "Hello, how are you?" to any customer who sees them.

7. Customers should never feel they are interrupting an employee, have to wait for an employee to finish a story, or stand and listen to the owner's instructions to an employee on work to be completed. The customer comes first.

8. All employees should be identified as such. It doesn't matter whether it's a name tag or special outfit, the customer should be able to readily identify who is an employee.

9. Don't do the customer a favor. Don't begrudge the customer. Employees should understand a customer complaint or problem is an opportunity to make an advocate for your store.

10. No employee should say to a customer, "That's not my job," or "That's not my department." Even if that is so, the employee must take the customer to someone who can answer the question.

11. Salespeople must be trained in product knowledge and core customer knowledge. First, train salespeople on all the core items and who the core customers are.

The big retailers have the hardest time institutionalizing a positive attitude and commitment to the customer. Their very bigness and bureaucratic ways fight against a customer orientation. This is their Achilles' heal, their weak spot, their poison. They have yet to figure an antidote. Any Main Street retailer who accepts employee indifference is missing the best opportunity to differentiate their business from the national chains.

The issue of employee indifference is really one of attitude and imitation. If the owner is overheard saying, "She is a stupid customer. . . ." or decides when a customer is important and when not, the employees will do likewise.

A positive employee attitude comes from training, discipline, and imitating management who must follow the rules they institute. There can be no exceptions to the commitment to the customer.

In the next chapter, Don't Be Overserviced, I will cover the need for and how to implement a solid training program for your employees.

◌ "IF WE DON'T PRICE IT, THEY'LL BE FORCED TO ASK."

Price everything.

Where appropriate and needed, have signs that explain the product to the customer, in the customer's terms, not in industry mumbo jumbo. Ask yourself, "Can the customer make an informed decision about this product *without* any sales help?" If the answer is no, include signage. The reasons are these: The customer is in a hurry; the customer is product ignorant, but wants to learn about the product; and most customers believe the written word more than a sales pitch. A customer who wants more information or decides to buy will ask for a salesperson.

The third part of this poison is disorganized product presentation. Customers do not like to hunt for products, especially if they don't understand how products are organized. By and large, the big stores do an excellent job organizing their products. It makes sense to the customer since it is laid out in a logical way. Even if all customers might not agree to the logic, the use of overhead signage makes the job much easier and far more convenient than the product search that starts with, "You take this half of the store and I'll try to find a salesperson. . . ."

The Main Street retailer should use the listen-naively sessions to determine how to improve the organization of the products. Core customers know how they want to look for products. Follow their lead.

Do everything to make it easier for the customer to shop: more information, logical organization, and price everything.

◊ "OUR STORE HAS THAT LIVED-IN LOOK."

Having a comfortable store is one thing, but dirty and disorganized is quite another. If the store is dirty or unkempt, it is unforgivable and an insult to your customers. Dirty is not charming. The store should be clean and not shopworn. It should be every employee's job to maintain the selling area. Each employee must be assigned a specific area to keep clean. The last thing employees should do before going home is clean their area.

This is so basic, but many retailers don't give it the attention it deserves. Cleanliness becomes the we'll-get-to-it-tomorrow project. Only discipline will correct the problem. Customers will not give you high marks for keeping the store clean since they consider it the minimum acceptable standard for a retail store. Don't lose customers because the store is not presentable.

Another part of the lived-in-look poison is the temptation of Main Street retailers to fill every bit of available display space with product, and then to cheat and start putting goods in the aisles, up the wall, and hanging from the cash register. That approach to display is a throwback to the days of delicatessen marketing. It is uninviting, makes it difficult to get around the store, and creates confusion. Give aisle space to the customers, not to merchandise.

Fewer product types, with a wider assortment of sizes, colors, and brands displayed well, is always more appealing than stacking stuff everywhere because you just had to buy it but have no place to display it.

⊘   OVERPROMISED AND UNDERDELIVERED

Big national retailers suffer from this poison. In an effort to get customers' attention, retailers state and imply promises in their advertising about lowest price, immediate stock availability, excellent service, product warranty, and store guarantee. It might be false advertising. In most cases, it's hype. The big retailer wants to tell customers everything they might want to hear, even though the retailer can't come close to keeping all these promises. Anything to get the customers into the store. Call this delicatessen advertising—a bunch of different promises of price and customer service greatness, but none kept. It disappoints many customers.

We live in an overpromised, overhyped, overstated retail world. Claims of the biggest inventory, widest assortment, best warranty, lowest price, and world-class service are so commonplace that they are unbelievable. They fall on deaf ears because no store can keep all these "est" (big*gest*, low*est*, etc.) promises.

The Main Street retailer's goal should be to promise only those benefits their core customers want, and to overdeliver consistently on those promises. Be better than the competition in a few things that are important to core customers. They will think the store is very good, and that is the surest way to fight the big stores and create advocates.

◊ THE LAW OF LOWERED EXPECTATIONS

Should the Main Street retailer give good service if no one else is? Should the Main Street retailer change promotional displays every month if no one else is? Many would suggest the answer to those questions is No. I hear these lines, "Why try to give better service? The customer won't pay for it." "Change the displays all you want, the customer isn't going to give you a dime more for your efforts." Nonsense. Those words are spoken by a retailer who has never committed to service or compelling displays. The retailer suffers from the poison of lowered expectations.

Any retailer who aims to meet, but not exceed, the average standards of all retailers in their marketplace sets into motion the law of lowered expectations. The average becomes the benchmark or goal for performance. Over time the customer comes to think this is the best it can be. "Why fight it?" the customer asks. The retailer believes they are doing just fine: "The customer doesn't want anything special. We do the same as the big stores when it comes to (service, delivery, store hours, etc.)."

The antidote for the poison of lowered expectations is always to have your core customer set the standards for performance and benefits delivered. The customer's perception of reality and their wishes or expectations for store improvement are the only standards you should meet.

Conclusion

Your store is only as good as your last complaint.

When you justify what you're doing by suggesting that other stores don't do it any better, you begin to suffer from the delusions of adequacy. The antidote to any of these poisons is to listen naively to your core customers and look to all retailers, not just those that are direct competition. If they do it well, adapt the idea and make it yours.

There should be one goal in retail: to find new and better ways to serve your customer. Your customers will catch your excitement and become your advocates.

14

DON'T BE OVERSERVICED

Customer service, in its broadest definition, is the single most potent advantage the Main Street retailer has over *all* national chain stores. Except for Nordstrom, I believe customer service is the biggest weakness of all national chains. Each big store has individual weaknesses, but it is my view that all deliver no better than mediocre customer service. Interestingly enough, many customers believe that "national chain" and "customer service" is an oxymoron. The customer's perception is that if you're a big store, good customer service is sacrificed for other benefits that the store can better execute.

Don't get me wrong, all the national chains work diligently to improve their customer service, but they are unwilling to give the salespeople and all frontline personnel who have contact with the customer the freedom and discretionary power to make decisions to help the customer. In the name of control and policy, management will not give those employees who deal with customers the authority to decide. Without that authority, customer service becomes slow and bureaucratic. Sears can change the name of "salespeople" to "associates," something it stole from Nordstrom, but without the power to really help the customer, the associate is just a cog in the Sears bureaucratic wheel.

The biggest problem for the national chains is that good customer service comes from the attitude and competence of employees. None of them has figured out how to clone 40,000 customer-service-minded employees. In place of cloning, the national chains have turned to technology to improve service and reduce cost. The national chains might have reduced their cost, but few think the "hit one and the pound sign for your credit balance. . ." is improved customer service. Perhaps the only real benefit to the customer is improved manual dexterity!

Customer service is the arena for the Main Street retailer to win the tug-of-war for customers. The customer's perception of the value of buying from the Main Street retailer is personal, believable customer service. Any Main Street retailer who has not fully taken advantage of their inherent strength of delivering good customer service will never reach their potential for success.

Many small retailers look at the successful, bigger Main Street retail store or national chain and say, "They're so big, they can afford (fill in the blank: personal customer service, low price, TV advertising, etc.)." That thinking is wrong. Wal-Mart did not start off with higher prices, because it couldn't buy in bulk. And as it got successful, it didn't decide to become the low-price general retailer. It started with low prices just as Nordstrom started with excellent customer service. That is how it got big.

The Main Street retailer will be successful and as big as it wants to get with better customer service. A basic part of any Main Street retail marketing effort must be improved customer service. It can and should be the cornerstone of any program to keep customers and create advocates.

This chapter offers the four steps to successful customer service:

1. Nordstromize service.
2. Mess up—Fess up.
3. Find the "nice" customer.
4. Thank customers, reward employees.

NORDSTROMIZE CUSTOMER SERVICE

DEFINITION
To deliver *consistently* good customer service as defined by the customer. To make customer service the mission of the Main Street retail store.

That definition might seem to be a very modest goal, but it is not. Consistently good service is rare in the retail and service industries. Any Main Street retailer who commits to my definition of customer service will deliver good customer service, create many advocates for their store, and be the envy of all retailers in their town. That's excellent.

Customer service has been written and talked about by more people in corporate America with less tangible results than anything else I can think of. Even with special service models, organizational matrices, and passionate exhortations to be the service leader, the quality of customer service continues to decline. Do Americans think service has improved in America? Americans answer with a resounding, No!

The national chains cannot institutionalize good, consistent customer service, and far too many Main Street retailers have succumbed to the poison of lowered expectations. Good customer service can only be attained if the Main Street retailer defines the company's goal in terms of customer satisfaction and retention, not dollars and cents.

If all business issues, and I mean all, are viewed against this commitment to customer service, the Main Street retailer will go a long way to inculcating the employees with good customer service habits.

Good customer service will come from embracing the Trivers Principles of Marketing. Good customer service is simply doing good marketing. They are really one and the same. The better you are at applying the Trivers Principles of Marketing, the better your company will deliver good customer service. Marketing starts with customers, not technology. So does customer service. Good marketing ends with satisfied customers who tell their friends, and so does good customer service.

The first step to Nordstromize the Main Street retail store is to know what the core customer expects. If the core customer doesn't care about some element of customer service, neither should the store. As in marketing, good customer service starts with listening naively to the customer. I suggested in Section III, Finding Customers, that all Main Street retailers should implement a monthly listen naively session with 10 core customers (pages 212–213). Part of the monthly meetings should always be concerned with customer service and what the customer expects. This should be an ongoing process. Some aspect of customer service should be discussed each month. As the core customer defines and redefines customer service, so does the Main Street retailer.

But just doing what the core customer says is only meeting their expectations. The next step is to include all employees and figure out how to enhance the customer's service idea. The Main Street retailer must be sure they can achieve the customer's idea and, with the employees' help, find small ways to improve and expand on the initial idea. When the store improves the customer service and adds its own pleasant surprises, it makes the service memorable. Memorable customer service creates advocates.

Let me give you an example of enhancing the customer's service idea or adding a pleasant surprise to customer service. United Parcel Service (UPS) is in the delivery business. On-time delivery, defined by the customer, is its mission, and UPS always asks its customers what improvements they would like. UPS went to Saturday delivery at customers' request. But the added pleasant surprise to their on-time delivery is that all UPS delivery personnel run from the truck to the retailer. Always. That single act has a more powerful effect on customers' perception than all the advertising in the world.

Good customer service comes from a collaboration between customers and employees, through old-fashioned teamwork. That collaboration creates a customer-service attitude among employees and a wish of all employees to excel at meeting the customer's expectations and taking it one step further with a special, memorable act.

How does the small retailer establish a service strategy and make customer service the mission of the store? Customer service is a mushy word. How does the retailer make it tangible? Reread the section on Retailer Indifference, especially Marketing Principle 2 on pages 243–244, that says, "Marketing is part of every employee's job." That is a good start for a customer-service strategy. I would add also:

1. Dress code.
2. Definition of acceptable customer service, like, "We will strive to satisfy and delight our customers. If we have not, we will redouble our efforts."

3.   Establish length of time to resolve any complaint, and at what dollar level the complaint resolution must be approved by the owner.
4.   Assign customer-service functions to nonsales employees.
5.   Establish a weekly 15-minute training session called "The Customer is Right." Review complaints, kudos from customers, and new ideas to better serve the customer. This should be fun, positive, and constructive. Don't let any, "Can you believe what Mrs. Smith wanted us to do?" be part of this. Give out small gifts or awards for ideas, extra effort displayed, or thank-you notes received.

By establishing a simple customer-service strategy rooted in positive employee behavior, the Main Street retailer will create the essence of Nordstrom: consistent, good customer service and small, memorable acts that make the customer feel special. And it is always downplayed—no bragging, no hype, no "Aren't we special?" *Underpromised but overdelivered customer service is the essence of keeping customers.*

MESS UP—FESS UP

Every Main Street retailer understands the need to resolve all complaints. Beyond resolution, there are two additional factors the Main Street retailer must get right: speed of resolution and attitude.

Speed is critical when handling a customer complaint. Satisfaction delayed is not satisfying. There is a simple rule about the amount of time it takes to resolve a problem: *The time taken to resolve a problem is in inverse proportion to the customer's satisfaction.*

Advocates are born from problems resolved quickly. To borrow a phrase, "To err is human, to fix the mistake immediately is divine and everybody will know of thy greatness." But to resolve the same problem over a long period of time is unforgivable, and customers won't forgive, nor will they forget. Resolve the problem quickly.

Quick resolution requires that employees be allowed to handle many problems and figure out a solution. Many store owners don't like to give up controlling the cost of resolving a complaint. Certainly, over a certain dollar level, the owner should be involved in the resolution, but most of the complaints will not be at that level and employees should have the training, support, and trust of the owner to resolve the problem. All problems should not flow to the top. It will slow the process and frustrate the customer. The store becomes a mini Sears, where control creates paralysis. It's not the way to keep customers and build advocates.

Nordstrom has one written rule for all salespeople on providing Nordstrom-quality customer service: "Use your good judgment in all situations." Now that's trust! Nordstrom knows customers will be more satisfied if the first person they talk to resolves the problem than if they get the same resolution, but had to talk to three people. Nordstrom also knows that a problem resolved quickly costs less.

Time taken to resolve a problem is in direct proportion to the cost to the store. The longer it takes to resolve a customer complaint, the less happy the customer will be and the more it will cost the store. That's why the Main Street retailer must train employees to solve customer complaints. It's cost-effective and helps create advocates.

Any supplier who is not committed to quick resolution of customer complaints should not be a supplier for the Main Street retailer. In many cases, the Main Street retailer has to turn to the supplier for help (repair, replacement, or an allowance). The supplier must be willing to resolve the complaint quickly or face hurting the Main Street retailer's reputation. No supplier is worth that.

Attitude is as important as speed of resolution. The attitude of the store owner is of the utmost importance. If the store owner grouses about the unreasonable or stupid customer, employees will do the same. Again, the store owner must lead by example. A customer complaint must be viewed as an opportunity to create an advocate.

As I mentioned before, an upset or dissatisfied customer who gets the problem resolved quickly and happily will be a bigger advocate than

*if someone never had a complaint. That attitude must permeate the re-
tail store.*

You as a customer know that an employee's attitude determines what kind of experience you'll have resolving a complaint.
If the employee is actually happy you are providing a chance to
fix a problem, you get less demanding and confrontational and
appreciate their sincerity. (I'll bet the first thing that comes to mind
is whether the person would consider working for you!)

I read about a Bank One executive who teaches his employees
to "run to the problem." I love that phrase.

*The Main Street retail store should have employees who enjoy run-
ning to the problem, not away from it. That attitude must come from
the top.*

After any problem has been resolved, a letter should go out
to customers from the store owner, thanking them for the opportunity to correct the problem.

FIND THE "NICE" CUSTOMER

If Mess Up—Fess Up is about reaction to a customer complaint,
Find the "Nice" Customer is about taking action. As you recall,
the "nice" customer is the one who does not complain to the store,
but quietly resolves never to return. It is important to have a system
in place to try to find the nice customer and get that customer to
explain their complaint with your store. This is a very difficult task.
The nice customer does not want to make a fuss, he just wants to
fade away, never to return.

I'll bet you've been a nice customer. I know I have. As a
business traveler, I will get irritated with a hotel and resolve not
to return. When I get to the desk to check out, the employee will
ask, "How was your stay?" On most occasions I say, "Fine." I'm
being a nice customer, and I'm not coming back. On one such
occasion, the clerk said, "What can we improve in our hotel so
your next visit will be more enjoyable?" I said, "Oh, everything
was fine." She said, "Mr. Trivers, if you're a businessman and
travel a lot, you know there are things we could improve." I told

her, chapter and verse. When I got home, I received a letter from the general manager, specifying what action the hotel had taken about my complaints. Wow, was I impressed!

On reflection, what really impressed me was that the hotel found a way to find the nice customer and get him to complain. So the question is: How do you get a nice customer to become a complaining customer so you can resolve the problem and gain an advocate? I suggest the following:

For big-ticket retailers

1. Send a thank-you card to every customer and enclose a questionnaire about the buying experience. Figure 14-1 is an example of a card used by Abbey Carpet.
2. Have a nonsalesperson call those customers who do not respond. Some of those could be nice customers. Script the introduction. I suggest following the type of lead-in that the clerk at the hotel used. Play to the customer's knowledge of good service.

Small-ticket retailers

1. At the point of purchase, all salespeople should get as many names and addresses as possible. For those people, mail the same type of thank-you card and questionnaire.
2. Of those who did not respond to the questionnaire, call every third one, or more. There are some nice customers in the nonrespondents group.
3. For those from whom you can't get the name, place the questionnaire/card in the bag, postage-paid and self-addressed. Some nice customers might have a change of heart and tell you their feelings about your store.
4. If the store has high traffic, have the employee at the cash register ask customers, "What is the one thing in this store you would like us to improve." Do this twice a year for a two-week period. I know you'll get some silly answers, but you'll see a pattern of things that should be improved. You'll have to assume that some nice customers feel the same way.

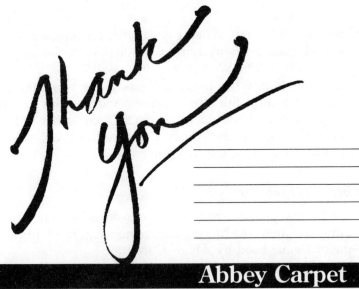

Abbey Carpet

America's choice, at your neighborhood store.

We take pride in our work and are constantly striving to maintain our high quality.
Would you help us by taking a minute to answer the questions? Thank You.

Were we responsive to your needs...	Excellent		Good	Unsatisfactory	
Before the job?	5	4	3	2	1
During the job?	5	4	3	2	1
After the job?	5	4	3	2	1
Was the job... Started on time?	5	4	3	2	1
Completed on time?	5	4	3	2	1
Left clean?	5	4	3	2	1
Did we do everything we agreed to do?	5	4	3	2	1
Were you satisfied with the price and value of the job we did?	5	4	3	2	1
Was the salesman helpful, courteous?	5	4	3	2	1
Was the installer helpful, courteous?	5	4	3	2	1
Would you consider us for future projects?	5	4	3	2	1

Over 1,000 Styles and Colors

Comments _____

May we use your name as a reference on future jobs? _____

Signature_____ Date _____ Phone _____

Abbey Carpet

America's choice, at your neighborhood store.

Figure 14-1. Thank-you card.

Obviously, finding the nice customer at a store that sells small-ticket items is harder, but you must try.

The Main Street retailer must find more than one way for the customer to complain and the store must resolve the complaint quickly. Those once unhappy, now very happy customers will tell their friends that the store really cares. *Always asking the customer how you can improve and gaining a reputation for a store that responds to problems is the best way to find nice customers and make them happy advocates.*

THANK CUSTOMERS, REWARD EMPLOYEES

Striving for and achieving good customer service is the smart way to thank customers in a special way. After the salesperson has said, "Thank you" at the point of sale, there should be other "Thank yous" after the sale:

1. Always thank the customer for bringing a problem to the store's attention.
2. When the problem is resolved, thank the customer for their patience.
3. Immediately after resolving the problem, the store should send a thank-you letter from the owner, even if the owner resolved the problem.
4. For any large sale, and all sales by big-ticket retailers, a thank-you card and a service questionnaire should be sent, with some personal note. Don't just sign the card.
5. When the customer-service questionnaire is returned, thank the customer again with a card. You can never overdo saying, "Thank you."
6. Repeat customers should receive a thank-you card, regardless of the size of the order.
7. Any correspondence or bill should always include, "Thank you for shopping at . . . ."

Simple courtesy will go a long way to building a good customer-service program. In our highly automated, hurried-up society, the Main Street retailer who takes the time to teach employees to say "Thank you" on many different business occasions will be handsomely rewarded. But the employees also must be rewarded for their efforts.

The core belief for most practitioners of good service is that customer service is only as good as employee morale. The better the store owner treats the employees, the better chance the store has of meeting its service goals and creating an image of a true, customer-service retail store. That feeling of strong company morale is what big companies have not institutionalized, and it is something many retailers don't pay attention to, but they must if they want to build a reputation for good customer service and intelligent small-business marketing.

Good customer service will come only from the company that believes in its employees. If that feeling is exhibited from the top, good customer service will flourish. Otherwise, all customer-service programs and policies will be for naught. I don't think I've ever been to a store where I could not tell how the employees were being treated—I just looked at how the employees were treating the customers. The direct correlation between employee morale and customer service really is that obvious. The heart of any retail store is the customer and the soul is the employee. They form the being of the store.

Obviously, this book does not include an employee manual, but let me give you my observations on the power of making all employees part of the customer-service effort. After customer service, the next most overused but underutilized business phrase is "empower." By now, all of corporate America should be muscle-bound, but most employees don't have a sense of ownership, hence the mediocre customer service. United Airlines almost admits in its recent advertising that before the 55,000 employees became owners of the airline, the employees were indifferent to customers.

How do you make employees part of the solution, not the problem? Can they be empowered? Yes, but the Main Street retailer must give them real, decision-making power and reward their efforts. Here are the Trivers's half dozen, but fully baked, ideas:

1. The owner must lead by example. Under no circumstances should any employee ever hear the owner say, "I'm so tired of these dumb customers. . ." or anything like that.
2. The owner must be a coach instead of a dictator.
3. Establish the Nordstrom rule as the only rule for resolving any issue with the customer: "Use your good judgment." Good judgment is not to run to the boss all the time. No recriminations for bad judgment—use training instead.
4. Reward with regular training sessions on product, customer service, and operations. Knowledge is power and empowerment.
5. Reward employees who "run to the problem."
6. Reward employees who add small ways to make the customer-service experience positively memorable.

Delivering good customer service is not easy. It's not just a question of saying "Thank you" all the time and having happy employees, it really is a question of how to bring all the parts of good customer service together in a coherent plan. That's just what Trivers did at Trivia Carpets by Trivers.

Trivia Carpets by Trivers

Trivers knew he acted like a dictator, he just thought he was a benign dictator. Decisions flowed down from the dictator while employees made few decisions on their own. He felt the company gave good customer service, but that was all it was, a feeling, since he had never asked his customers how they rated Trivia Carpets' customer service.

Trivers realized in the listen-naively sessions that he was holding every month with 10 core customers that good customer service was an important benefit the customers were seeking. How could he improve the store's overall customer service? One thing became clear: He knew the commitment to a real, personable, and sustainable customer-service program was going to mean change for everyone, including himself. But you don't just mandate change. It must be worked on, one step at a time, and reviewed constantly to ensure the change is what was intended.

This is how Trivers integrated the different facets of customer service into the initial customer-service and marketing program, the goal of which is to create advocates and keep customers:

1. Trivers decided to change. Calls were no longer screened. No meeting was too important if a customer called. He encouraged salespeople to resolve complaints without running to him, within certain dollar guidelines. He no longer disparaged a customer. He treated customer complaints as an opportunity to create an advocate, not as a contest to fight an unfair and stupid customer. He tried to become a coach.

2. Trivers sat down with all of his suppliers and told them how long they had to resolve product complaints. Those that could not meet these standards were dropped as suppliers.

3. Now he was ready for the employee meeting. Only after he had the suppliers' agreement and had started his own personal change was he ready for the meeting to initiate a full customer-service program. The meeting would not have been believable to the employees without a demonstration of a change in behavior of Trivers prior to the meeting. This way, the response was, "Hey, he's serious, he's even changing," as opposed to, "Looks like we have some more, 'Do as I say, not as I do stuff.'"

4. The thrust of the meeting was positive change, the way the customer wants. The store was going to practice customer service the way the customer would like, not the way a supplier wanted. The store was going to set new standards of customer service and reward achievement.

The proof of seriousness was the change the employees already saw in Trivers's behavior and he expected change from them, as well.

5. He gave employees assignments to complete in two weeks: a customer-service mission statement, program for phone etiquette, procedure to handle all complaints, thank-you program, dress code, and creative ideas to make customer service memorable.

6. All received a hat that said, "The Team." The hat was to be worn at all Friday "The Customer Is Right" customer-service meetings, which were to start after the employees completed their assignments on redefining Trivia Carpets' customer service.

7. Trivers was amazed by the response. He had tapped the employees' business and creative skills and they had delivered. (In the past, Trivers felt some employees spent all their energy on rumors. He now realized that that was his fault. Dictators rarely give the underlings a chance to be positive and build a team. Trivers used to complain about their complaining. Now he had a program that rewarded positive, creative ideas. Trivers was positive and employees returned the feeling and energy with great ideas for his store.)

8. Trivers blended the ideas into an orderly statement of the store's mission, including the behavior and procedures needed to achieve the goal.

9. Trivers started the Friday morning meetings. At each one, Trivers rewarded an employee for good customer service and ideas to improve the service. The prize was inexpensive and fun. Trivers wanted to get one new customer-service idea each Friday and also keep his team pulling in the same direction.

10. Trivers wrote a newsletter to all his customers describing what his company did about customer service. He included pictures of their initial meetings, hats and all. (Trivers realized that companies make many internal decisions that affect customers and then never tell the cus-

tomer about the change. Customers love to hear how you're changing the business for them.)

For Trivers, delivering customer service the way the customer wanted it was all about change—in his day-to-day business behavior, in giving his employees decision-making responsibility, in the attitude of the employees. This new approach to customer service did not happen overnight; real change always takes longer. There were some casualties. Some employees did not want to change and they were asked to leave. His Friday-morning meetings are a regular part of employee training, and he continues to solicit ideas from his core customers. Nordstrom would be envious.

Conclusion

The single weakest marketing element for almost all national retail chains is customer service. It has deteriorated for so long that many customers now have lowered expectations of what is acceptable customer service. Even though they have been numbed by mediocre customer service, they can recognize and will appreciate good customer service. It is incumbent upon the Main Street retailer to make customer service a powerful strength. It will be rewarded.

The rewards will not come without some real personal costs. Most store owners will have to change their behavior. That's not easy. Most employees will have to redirect their energies to the customer and away from focusing on internal operations. That's not easy. An active training program must be ongoing, never to stop. That's not easy.

Consider the rewards: An army of advocates will tell everyone they meet about the special treatment customers receive at your store.

Word-of-mouth marketing is the power of positive gossip.

15

ACT DIRECT, BE DIRECT

Keeping customers is about delivering superior benefits to your core customers. It is also about thanking and treating them in special ways so that many will become advocates for your Main Street store. Like everything in retail marketing, ways of treating the core customer special must be disciplined and repeated.

This is not a question of altruism. It is very smart marketing to communicate, after the sale, with customers. It is the least expensive and most productive way to build repeat business and customer loyalty. At the same time, the Main Street retailer should ask these loyal customers to help find new customers for the store. That is the key to "Act Direct, Be Direct."

Every program to keep customers also should have a "finding customers" component.

Act Direct, Be Direct takes its lead from the best direct-marketing companies and the smart Main Street retailers who truly know their customers. General advertising informs the core and all other potential customers of an event or sale that is taking place at the store. This type of communication is not selective—everyone knows. Act Direct, Be Direct is selective communication primarily directed to the core customers and occasionally to all customers who have purchased from the store. The very combination of direct and selective communication makes the core customer feel special and happy about their relationship with the store. Even if the core customer cannot attend the function or do what is suggested in the letter, the store will have created the sense that it cares about the customer. That's how advocates are created.

Act Direct is about building the store's database and improving the Main Street retailer's knowledge of the core customer.

Be Direct contains ideas for special events or communications for existing customers, only. Running those events completes the definition of smart marketing and begins the process of finding customers. The cycle continues.

ACT DIRECT: THE DATABASE

Database is computer talk for "knowledge about the customer." Earlier in this book, I told you that a computer was a necessity for the Main Street retailer. It is not something to buy after the store grows. The computer is an essential tool to help any store become bigger and more successful. If you want to keep customers, create advocates, and find more customers like your core customers, a computer and database file will make the process manageable, inexpensive, efficient, and disciplined.

A retail-store database starts with the names and addresses of all customers. From that, the pin-cluster analysis can be completed. That alone should go far toward improving the productivity of promotions and figuring out the best media to find more customers like the core customers. Names and addresses are only the beginning of a useful customer database. In addition to names and addresses, the database should include:

1. All products purchased. *The Database Advantage:* If the store wants to get rid of merchandise, it allows those customers who are frequent buyers of the products to be contacted by phone or postcard. If the store has received a new shipment of a specific type of product or brand, it allows those customers who are frequent buyers of the product or brand to be contacted. If the store is overstocked in a specific size or color, those customers who have bought the size or color can be told.

    When the information is collected by purchase, the store has the ability to communicate with the best customer to get rid of problem products, sizes, even colors. When new products arrive, the customer database file can be used to choose existing customers who might be interested in them, based on their buying habits. All this is done with the stroke of a computer key and it is the essence of keeping customers by better serving them.

2. How the purchases were paid for. *The Database Advantage:* The store can create payment-specific promotions. If VISA has a special deal, the store can communicate only with its VISA customers.

3. The purchase dates. *The Database Advantage:* The Main Street retail store can send out an anniversary card celebrating the first year of a business relationship. Sounds corny, but it works. Saying "Thank you" is always appreciated, especially if it is personalized, like an anniversary date. The store can select the one-time buyers, and ask them to revisit the store, or select the repeat customers for a special program.

Any Main Street retail database should include the basic information of name, address, products purchased, date of purchase, and form of payment. Armed with that information, the Main Street retailer can communicate with customers in a very personal and compelling way. It is one thing to run an ad shouting "Save 50%," and another to communicate with Ms. Jones directly and talk about what products she buys from your store and inform her of a new arrival of her favorite brand. The courtesy will impress Ms. Jones, the fact that you have remembered (thank you, computer) her favorite brand will astound her, and the fact that you asked her to bring a friend when she comes to the store will make her smile. Of course, she will want to show off a store that is so considerate to her special wants and needs.

The computer will enable any store to maintain and update essential customer information. Database software will enable any store to sort the information any way possible. Indeed, at the stroke of a key the store can access customer information, but the process of communicating with customers based on their buying habits must be disciplined.

To get the most out of a customer database, the store should consider using it for any opportunity or problem. The store will communicate with the right customers at the least cost, and the customers will appreciate the store for thinking of them. How will the Main Street retailer know who to communicate with? If customers bought a product or service in the past, they have a need for it and will be interested in anything about the product or service. It is nothing more sophisticated than that.

Turn to the customer database for these problems: serious overstock of running-line products; manufacturer drops product, size, or colors from their line; and slow sellers, or seasonal products still in inventory at the end of a season. Turn to the customer database for these opportunities: new stock of limited-supply product; new products or brands introduced; any in-store promotions not announced in the general media; new service or warranty for specific products; new credit program; and to announce an event or promotion in which the customer has previously participated. In each of these cases, if the Main Street retailer selects only those customers who have some history of buying the specific product, brand, or service, and communicates with them exclusively, the store will take care of the problem or expand an opportunity with the least effort and cost, and highest return.

The other part of the database program for the Main Street retailer is the list of names and addresses of prospective customers who live in the pin-cluster area of the core customers. When prospective customers buy from the store, they must be deleted from the prospective customer file and added to the customer file with all the purchase information.

Acting direct and using a database makes all the sense in the world. Why, then, is it used by *all* direct-marketing (catalog) companies and so few Main Street retailers? Is the customer database only important for those companies that don't have a store and don't have personal contact with the customers? Won't the Main Street retailer's customers find this type of communication obnoxious and unnecessarily intrusive?

Database marketing is marketing; everything else is playacting. I suspect retailers lull themselves into a self-satisfying, "We're doing just fine" complacency and mistakenly believe that daily customer interaction can suffice over real customer knowledge that can and should enhance the relationship with the customer. Smiling at a customer who is attending a community event might make the retailer feel good, but it is hardly knowing the customer and their buying habits.

The customer will rarely feel that special communications to them are intrusive or unwanted. Use a postcard for problems, like liquidating problem inventory. It should be preprinted and as simple as:

This Bargain's for You

WOW! We are taking a BIG markdown on your favorite _____ . Quantities are limited, so please visit us or call as soon as possible. This bargain's for you. Thanks (handwritten) P.S. Bring along a bargain-loving friend!

For specific sale opportunities, use a larger envelope or letter which is printed for the specific event. An inexpensive graphics package for the computer can do the job. Assign one employee to handle the different communications and maintain the list. Everything can be done in-house, even the printing if the quantity is small enough.

Every time the store is faced with a problem or opportunity, the first question should be, "Are there some customers who would appreciate knowing about this?" Unless no one has ever bought the product before, the answer will be, "Yes." Product problems are changed to, "This bargain's for you." Opportunities are expressed in the idiom of the customer: "We have just received a new shipment of your favorite (brand name) casual clothes. Your excellent taste is shared by many others. . . ." Make these communications short and direct.

Conclusion

The key to a successful database is discipline. One employee should handle updating the file (deleting and adding names, changing addresses) and creating the communication pieces. It must be an ongoing process, with mailings occurring on a regular basis, and every mailing should ask the core customer to bring along a friend or neighbor.

Database marketing is marketing the way the customer wants it: personal and always thinking about the customer's well-being. That's the way the customer perceives this form and method of communication, and the customer is always right. Why would you do otherwise?

BE DIRECT: ASK FOR THE CUSTOMERS' HELP

People like to give their advice on most anything. They like to know that the advice is being considered, and are absolutely enthralled if the advice is taken. This applies to the Main Street retailer, not just politicians. What better way is there to learn how to communicate in the idiom of the customer than to listen to the customer in their idiom?

Soliciting core customer advice occurs during the monthly listen-naively sessions, but all customers should be asked, once a year, to grade the store's performance. The customers' ideas are reported back to the store in a quarterly newsletter (see the following section) and customers are informed when ideas are implemented.

The "Customer Help" questionnaire should be one page, both sides, professionally organized and printed. You can use your computer graphics to do this. The questionnaire should include:

1. First ask to see if the store is suffering from delusions of adequacy. Ask these questions:
    a. Do we have a wide enough assortment of our key items (list them)? If not, what do you suggest?
    b. How many times last year were we out of stock of advertised items? Regular items?
    c. Our goal is to answer the phone by the third ring. How many times did we fail to do so? Were you put on hold for more than 10 seconds? How many times? Was any employee in a meeting and not available when you wanted to speak to them? How many times did that occur?
    d. Do all employees who come in contact with you greet you?

e. Please rate our salespeople for product knowledge and courtesy.

f. Are all products priced? Is the product presentation and signage adequate for you to make a decision?

g. Are aisles clear of products and any unnecessary clutter?

h. Do we live up to the expectations we create in all our advertising? If not, explain.

2. Have the customers rate your customer service in detail, by asking them more than one question. Explain your store's commitment to customer service, how you define it, and what the customer should expect from your store. Ask them to rate your store against other stores. Ask them what areas need improvement and for suggestions on how to do it.

3. Include other questions unique to your industry or town.

4. End the questionnaire with an open-ended, "Tell us what irks you about us."

5. Promise anonymity. Don't color code or use any other method to decipher where the customer lives.

6. Include an incentive for response. Tie the incentive to names of friends of the customer who the customer thinks would like to know more about your store. It works like this: For each friend listed, the customer earns one ticket for a drawing. The more friends, the more tickets. Check the list of friends against your database and mail a brochure to those not on your database. Include a personal note explaining why the brochure is being mailed. Add their name to your prospective customer data file.

The Main Street retailer should mail the questionnaire in January each year. A 25% return can be expected if a self-addressed, stamped envelope is included. This simple, direct approach to improving the retail operation helps the Main Street retailer stay close to customers and to use their creative energies to guide his business. That is very smart marketing.

BE DIRECT: QUARTERLY NEWSLETTER

The quarterly newsletter is an inexpensive way to stay in front of customers and keep them interested in your business. I would set it up as follows:

1. Hire a local newspaper reporter to learn about your business and write the four newsletters. Newspaper reporters are notoriously underpaid; they'll be most grateful and won't charge you much.
2. Each newsletter should be 8½″ × 11″, folded to 5½″ × 8″. Use black print and one color for logo and graphic interest.
3. Create four sections: (a) new products, brands, or services; (b) employee profile with picture; (c) customer's comments or suggestions that have been compiled; (d) space for customer comments, and name and address of customer's friends who should know something about the store—this should always be the last page.
4. Use two to three pictures in each edition.
5. The first edition of each year should have a special insert exclusively devoted to the questionnaire sent out in January. Share all the comments, good and bad.
6. In the other three editions, update the progress being made to correct any problems customers reported about. Include this information in section c of the newsletter.
7. The newsletter should be fun and informative.
8. Always print more copies than are needed for buying customers. Select 200 to 300 prospective customers from the pin-cluster area and send the newsletter to them with a note explaining the newsletter and why they should visit the store.

Most retailers don't use newsletters because it means writing and overseeing something they are not familiar with, but that is not a good reason to reject them. If you find a local reporter or someone who can write well, the newsletter is a great way to stay in front of your customers. That's what keeping customers is all about: communicating with your customers other than when they buy from you.

With the printing overruns (additional copies for prospective customers), the newsletter becomes an excellent tool to find new customers. A building remodeler in Medford, Oregon, Brad Youngs Construction, sent out occasional newsletters, but never to prospective customers. In July 1995, Brad mailed 325 to existing customers (they had dealt with Youngs Construction in the last seven years) and another 250 to prospective customers in his core pin-cluster areas. The first call he received was from a designer who had used Youngs Construction as a consumer 11 years ago, and now was looking for reputable remodelers for seven projects she was completing for her design company. She had forgotten Brad Youngs Construction, since Brad made no effort to stay in front of his customers on a regular basis. Luckily, his newsletter reminded the designer of his company and he was asked to bid on all seven projects.

That is not a story about dumb luck. It shows the real value of regularly communicating with your customers, and the penalty if you do not. Even if Brad Youngs Construction does not receive one more lead from the mailing, he knows the newsletter idea is a success. Brad will mail them every quarter, without fail, and reap the rewards!

BE DIRECT: THE REALLY PRIVATE SALE

People like to be part of something exclusive. The Really Private Sale is just for customers who have purchased from you. Of course, they will be asked to bring a friend, but no one else will be invited.

This is what I would do:

1. Run the sale once a year, same date every year.
2. It should run after regular store hours.
3. Announce the event in the newsletter and an imaginative direct-mail piece. Be sure the direct-mail piece includes an incentive to bring a friend.

4. Have a nice gift for all who come: a rose for the woman, or something with the store's name on it.

5. Consider joining with a nonprofit organization to benefit them in some way.

6. This does not have to be a dressy affair. You just want to say, "Thanks" in a low-key, neighborly way. However, all employees should be dressed in similar-looking attire.

7. There needs to be something special going on with products or brands, beyond price reduction: a new display, preview of the fall line, new brand being introduced, etc.

8. Do not expect big sales from this. You want to say, "Thank you" in a creative way. You'll get the sales later.

9. Add all the names of the guests into your customer file and treat them as buying customers, even if they didn't buy anything.

It well might be that if you've already run a private sale using your pin-cluster markets, you don't want to participate in another private sale. That's understandable, but you should have an event for customers to thank them.

Try a picnic. Ben and Jerry's Ice Cream has a national picnic for customers, just to thank them. Saturn suggests that its dealers put on a picnic to thank their customers and offer training about repairing the car. The only drawback with a picnic is there is no opportunity to sell any products.

It does not matter what program you choose, but you should choose a simple, friendly way to say thanks. Remember, customers expect personal service. Exceed their expectation with a special event dedicated to buying customers only.

BE DIRECT: THE SHOPPING-BAG CAPER

This idea offers the Main Street retailer a great opportunity to keep customers involved in the store in a fun way. It works like this:

1. A vibrant shopping bag (make it any size you want, but it should be made out of plastic) is used for purchases over $30.

2. Employees suggest to customers that if they use the bag on a trip, to take a picture of themselves with the bag shown prominently.
3. Promise the customer that if they bring in the picture you will put it up on the Traveling Tote Board.
4. As the pictures come in, more customers will participate. All of a sudden, someone will bring in a picture of themselves standing on the wall of China holding your bag. People will want to outdo that, and so excitement and fun are created.

I like the shopping-bag caper. It creates the kind of fun, active communication that creates advocates.

Conclusion

The big stores are taking a larger share of the retail market with larger assortments and lower prices. Main Street retailers have been passive, worrying more about losing customers than building strategies for keeping customers.

Keeping customers is simple and should be fun. All it requires is a belief in and commitment to the smart definition of marketing: the process of finding and keeping customers.

All Main Street retailers I know believe they take care of their customers and they do, at point of sale. But most don't *after* the sale. That is what keeping customers is all about.

Keeping customers is the least expensive part of the marketing definition and can deliver the best results. In almost every act of keeping customers, you solicit names of prospective customers who are like your existing customers. That way, the cycle of success continues.

GETTING DOWN TO BUSINESS
Applying Marketing Principles to Your Business

Here's a checklist for Keeping Customers:

Delusions of Adequacy

1. Create a list of your customers' retail poisons. Have all employees do the same. Compile the 10 most important poisons.
2. Establish programs to guarantee the store doesn't poison its operation.

Don't Be Overserviced

1. Put together a complete program to be the best customer-service retailer in your town.

Act Direct, Be Direct

1. Commit to using your database for product liquidation and announcing important new product arrivals.
2. Set up two special programs to thank customers, by staying in touch.

INDEX